At Sunshine Coast's End
— The Broadstairs Story

by **NICK EVANS**

Bygone Publishing

FRONT COVER PHOTO: Broadstairs harbour and seafront c1970.

BACK COVER PHOTO: Viking Bay's safety boat awaits its next call for help in 1972.

Contents

Author's introduction

For several summers in the late 1960s and early 1970s my family hired one of the many concrete chalets on the verandahs of Viking Bay which meant we could enjoy the fine sands, the crashing waves, Punch & Judy, the nearby ice cream parlours and the occasional welsh rarebit at the Omar Café (which was next door to the Royal Albion Hotel). In my later teenage years, local hostelries would prove to be a different magnet.

Many thousands of visitors to Broadstairs will have similar memories of bucket and spade holidays in the town which, I hope, will be rekindled as you thumb through the pages of this book. Holidays, assisted by the arrival of the Victorian railway, raised the profile of Broadstairs considerably. It quickly turned from a sleepy fishing town to a seaside resort for the well-heeled, particularly once author Charles Dickens became a regular visitor and wrote some of his most famous work here.

A short distance away are the villages of Reading Street, Kingsgate and St Peter's – the latter being the more affluent partner to Broadstairs in centuries past – which, as you will see, all have their own places in the area's history.

Much of the material in this book has been drawn from my family's archive of feature articles, photographs and postcards, a large part of that created by my late father Bill Evans, a journalist, who, having grown up in Broadstairs before the Second World War, knew and loved the place a great deal. That material gives us an unbeatable insight into its history now.

I leave it to the words of Charles Pooter, the main character of George & Weedon Grossmith's Victorian comic novel, The Diary Of A Nobody, to sum it all up. When asked where he wishes to spend his summer holidays, he exclaims: "I don't think we can do better than Good Old Broadstairs!" Wise words indeed.

Nick Evans
Whitstable
September 2021

Early days on the eastern tip of England

Although it would not rise to prominence until writer Charles Dickens stayed for his holidays and the railway arrived in the 19th century, Broadstairs, whose coastline forms the second most easterly point of England, had long been a must-visit place.

Despite first appearances as somewhere small and heavily reliant on fishing, the village of Bradstow was a major anchorage for mariners of much larger vessels.

In 1514, the entire 700 strong crew of King Henry VIII's newly-built flagship, The *Henry Grace a Dieu* came ashore after mooring in the bay. They were there to seek a blessing at the shrine of Our Lady of Bradstow, Star of the Sea, venerated by mariners for at least the three previous centuries. (The shrine was set close to where the Chapel Bookshop and bar now stands in Albion Street).

Once blessed, the crew could feel more confident about putting to sea again for a safe voyage.

After that visit, which also included a grand feast

Broadstairs jetty is thought to be the oldest in England having been built in 1538 by local benefactor and shipbuilder George Culmer. The jetty was rebuilt in the early 19th century and it is seen here about 100 years later.

hosted by the locals, passing ships would lower their top flag in thanks for a safe voyage.

Six years after the King's crew visited, the chapel and shrine were lost in a raging storm which lasted several days, a surge tide sweeping away much of Bradstow itself.

Much of the immediate area was rebuilt by the Culmer

family, who ran extensive shipyards at one end of the bay. In 1538 – the year monasteries were being dissolved by the king – George Culmer built a pier, or jetty, creating a formal harbour. Two years later, he built what we know today as the York Gate, in Harbour Street. Originally known as Flint Gate, the arch supported heavy wooden doors to keep out marauding privateers intent on attacking the place.

During the 17th and 18th centuries it was smuggling that supported the lives of many in the area. Tobacco, brandy, lace and tea were favourite goods brought ashore at night, most notably through bays at Kingsgate and Joss Bay. In those times they were isolated places and well away from prying eyes, despite the best efforts of the outnumbered and outgunned Revenue men. The railway arrived in Broadstairs from London during the 1860s, near the end of a line running to Ramsgate via Margate and Faversham. Thanks to this track linking to an existing one at Ramsgate, passengers have long had the choice of travelling to the capital via Canterbury and Ashford if they choose.

For the next 100 years or so, and in spite of changes in

York Gate.
Broadstairs.

Lord Henniker restored the York Gate in 1795 as insurance against a French incursion and his name is borne in an inscription on one side of the stone work.

taste and fashion, Broadstairs became the resort of people wanting a quiet holiday in a select area. Generations of visitors, in the early days some arriving with a nanny and several children, have been welcomed to this sunniest of corners on the south coast. In the 20th century, many older people found Broadstairs an ideal place for enjoying their retirement years.

Broadstairs was the favourite destination of Charles

Pooter in George and Weedon Grossmith's The Diary of A Nobody. "I don't think we can do better than Good Old Broadstairs", he replied when asked where he would like to spend his summer holidays.

He was certainly able to relax while away from his banking job in London, only to be scorned by his son Lupin when donning a straw hat to walk along the parade. Pooter was equally contemptuous when he found Lupin had gone to 'a common sort of entertainment, given at the Assembly Rooms'.

The late 19th century of Mr Pooter was an era of bathing machines, long dresses, large hats and rolled parasols. It was a picture which would last until the First World War began in the summer of 1914 as indicated by an Edwardian town guide issued by the former Broadstairs & St Peter's Urban District Council.

Under the heading of 'amusements' it reads: 'Owing to the wise control exercised by the local authorities, Broadstairs is free from the objectionable forms of seashore entertainment which are met with in many coast towns. Nevertheless there is a sufficiency of al fresco amusements of the favourite type.....'

The sands, we are told, were never dull. Indeed the 'seashore on a sunny morning, thronged with happy children paddling in perfect security at the edge of the waves, presents a kaleidoscopic picture of singular animation and attractiveness.'

Savouring more of the Edwardian scene we learn: 'A first-class band plays beneath a shelter at the extremity

This Edwardian postcard shows donkeys about to carry their riders on another walk along the beach while, nearby, a group of youngsters builds a sandcastle. The chair would have had upturned lids from shoe polish tins attached to the base of each leg to stop it from sinking in the sand – an early deck chair perhaps?

The Sands.   Broadstairs.

of the picturesque pier. In the afternoon the Victoria Gardens are the rendezvous of music lovers who delight to lounge in the comfortable deck-chairs provided by the enterprise of the Band Committee.'

But there was night life too. Each evening there were performances in the seafront bandstand whose summer runs continued unbroken during the era between the two world wars.

For many years the town's concert hall was the Bohemia, set halfway down the hilly High Street, which was destroyed in a fire during the early 1960s. Previously known as the Lawn Garden but later becoming the home of the Bohemia Concert Party, it initially used a large awning for cover in sunshine and shower before becoming a more permanent structure.

In the earlier part of the 20th century a royal link with Broadstairs was forged through the physician of King Edward VII who owned York Gate House in Harbour Street. The young princes Edward, George and Henry and Princess Mary stayed there. A newspaper of the time reported the boy, who would become the Duke of Windsor, was 'full of boyish pranks and mischief. He loves to tumble about on the golden sands, to dig sand holes, to chase crabs and small fish which abound in the pools near the bay.' Their mother Queen Mary was a frequent, if unexpected, visitor and more than once the station master at Broadstairs would get a hurried phone call from Margate telling him: "The Queen is on the next train!"

A reflection very much of times past – and commonplace at seaside towns up and down the country – were the troupes of children's entertainers who

The ornate 1887 Victoria Jubilee bandstand was a focal point for many visitors wanting to relax lazily and watch the world go by in this early 1920s view.

performed daily on the beach during the summer. Long remembered is Harry Summerson, who for more than 50 years was Uncle Mack to thousands of youngsters. Although frowned upon now, he and his merry colleagues were usually black-faced for their performances on a special stage on the sands. Adults as much as children enjoyed the minstrels with their songs, sketches and cheerful patter.

Still in times before people discovered package holidays abroad, traditional Punch and Judy proved a big draw for children, 'Professor' Peter Butchard being the puppet theatre's impresario throughout the 1960s and 1970s.

In the mid 1960s, Jack Hamilton had made his mark on the Devon coast helping to revive the English folk music and dance scene there. He wanted to found his own festival somewhere in the south-east and when he arrived in Broadstairs, he knew he had found the perfect place.

After decades of continual growth, backed by public and private sponsorship, Broadstairs Folk Week has become one of the largest events of its kind in the country today. It brings to the town centre a near non-stop programme of music, singing and dancing appealing across the age range. For the pubs and bars of the town, it is the busiest week of the year – anything connected with folk music usually calls for ongoing

Broadstairs Folk Week has been held every August, with the exception of 2020, since 1965 and is now one of the biggest festivals of its kind in Britain. Here, the Hartley Mens Morris entertain in Pierremont Park c1991.

refreshment after all! The festival's value to the local economy is significant, bringing, in pre-pandemic times, an estimated near £3 million a year to the town.

Broadstairs has been fortunate to have, in the main, retained something of its select image, sandwiched as it is between Margate and Ramsgate. It still has much to offer to staycation visitors as well as those seeking a new lifestyle at sunshine coast's end. Long may that continue.

Promenading along the foreshore

Behind the line of trees lies King George VI Memorial Park – which was part of Ramsgate when this view was taken in the 1950s, looking along South Cliff Parade, Dumpton. Despite accusations of snobbery, Broadstairs would not take down the low wall fronting the trees and thus kept the two towns divided for walkers. A section of the wall was eventually demolished in the early 1970s when houses were built around the corner, out of this view, along Seven Stones Drive.

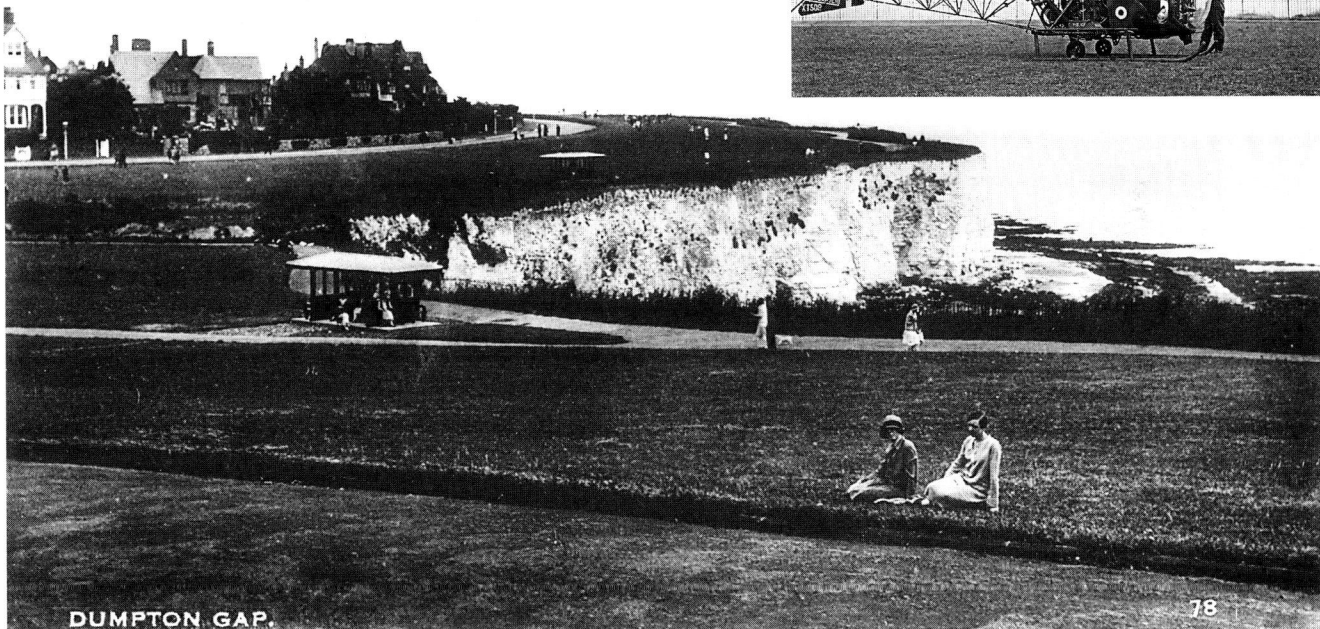

DUMPTON GAP.

78

Dumpton Gap was once known as Dodemayton and used by local farmers to collect seaweed from the beach which they then spread as fertiliser on their fields. In 1914 a submarine telephone cable was laid from here, across the Channel, to Ostend. The junction hut still stands at the top of the slipway. Inset: Walkers would have had quite a surprise in 1968 when an Army helicopter landed here for a time. It was on loan to local police, to test its suitability at landing in restricted spaces.

LITTLE CASTLEMERE

CASTLEMERE, BROADSTAIRS

Telephone : 1166

The Castlemere Hotel on the Western Esplanade was once run by Mrs Margaret Knight-Bruce and Miss Elizabeth Bennett. Composer Sir Richard Rodney Bennett was born here on 29 March 1936 – his mother choosing to be with her in-laws at the time. Little Castlemere was the overflow part of the hotel in 1949. Sir Richard died in New York on 24 December 2012, aged 76.

This postcard view of Louisa Gap was captured during the 1960s soon after the promenade and cliff defences had been completed. A decade before, the gap was popular with sand sculptors. People showed their appreciation by throwing coins down to them from the clifftop! Luckily, no one was injured. The clifftop scene offers a wide angle of Broadstairs seafront.

Louisa Gap, Broadstairs.

Louisa Gap is just a short walk from the main bay. Taken in the early 20th century, we can see how close the Grand Hotel was to the beach but stairs were not built down from the bridge until 1905. Originally known as Goodson Stairs, after a local farmer, the gap was renamed after singer Louisa Crampton, daughter of engineer Thomas who built the bridge in 1850.

The Grand Hotel Broadstairs

An Edwardian stylised view of the Grand Hotel set atop the cliffs of Louisa Bay. The town's premier hotel, it was built in 1882 for £78,000. The Grand boasted 110 bedrooms plus reading rooms, smoking rooms and billiard hall. In 1938 the hotel held four AA stars and a week's stay cost nine guineas (£9.45) per person. Later on, the hotel gave way to become the Grand Mansions apartments while the ballroom became the town's leading entertainment venue. It was demolished in the 1990s to make way for new flats.

utting Green and front, Broadst.

1551

A putting green has existed on the corner of Granville Road with Victoria Parade for around 100 years. Known these days as Lillyputt Mini Golf, it was run by Pat Regan in the 1950s when 18 holes cost just 6d. A decade before, Jack Nunn charged 4d (2p). Competitions, with prizes, between guest houses were a regular attraction.

An Isle of Thanet Tramway vehicle picks up a passenger on Victoria Parade before clattering around the corner to Granville Road. Trams ran between Westbrook, near Margate, and Ramsgate between 1901 and 1937 until East Kent's buses took over. The four-wheeled single bogie tramcars had been built in America and the company's main depot and works was at St Peter's.

THE BANDSTAND, BROADSTAIRS

Moving further along the road, we see an elderly lady being hauled in her bath chair by a young man in this early 20th century view. The crowd seems intent on gathering around the ornate 1887 Victoria jubilee bandstand for a concert. Across the bay, barges, possibly colliers, rest on the sand while the tide is out. The bandstand was rebuilt nearby on its present site in 1952.

Bracing sea air was a certainty as you walked along the promenade in Edwardian times. The Victoria Gardens were opened by Princess Louise in 1832 and have remained a focal point of many a clifftop walk ever since. Later on, the town council purchased the gardens which then became Broadstairs' first official park.

Mario Morelli opened his first ice cream parlour and cappuccino bar on the seafront at Broadstairs in 1932. Joe Morelli took over from his father in the 1950s and redeveloped the parlour in 1959, making it the first of its kind in Britain. For many, visiting Morelli's to sample its wide range of flavours of ice cream is an integral part of a visit to Broadstairs.

The black-knobbed circular ashtrays on the tables are the only real giveaways to the true age of this photo which was taken in 1959, soon after its enlargement by Joe Morelli. The ornate ceiling, the mirror-backed serving area and the Lloyd Loom chairs are still key features of the decor – Morelli's interior has changed little in over 60 years. Management passed to Joe's son Marino in 1972 and, since the late 1990s, the business has been led by Bibi Morelli who has expanded it into an international operation.

VelvaCream ice cream was synonymous with Morellis and this Austin van, with Joe and dog posing alongside, was a familiar sight around Thanet during the 1950s. Today, Morelli's has outlets around the world, making fresh gelato every day, in such far flung places as Dubai, Philippines, Gabon, Texas as well as in London's Covent Garden.

A history of Broadstairs is not complete without mention of Uncle Mack and his troupe of minstrels who entertained for many years. Uncle Mack, Harry Summerson, brought joy and laughter to Broadstairs between 1895 and 1948. He died in 1949. Public subscriptions paid for a memorial stone, located in Victoria Gardens, in 1950 when council Chairman Fred Salt and actress Annette Mills, of Muffin The Mule fame, who lived nearby, unveiled it before a big crowd. In recent years Thanet District Council has covered the stone with a wooden box following vandal attacks, including one on the box itself by a former councillor in June 2020.

19 BAY & SANDS LOOKING WEST, BROADSTAIRS.

Taken from the main steps down to the beach in the early 20th century, we can only guess at what the large crowd is enjoying. It's most likely to be Punch & Judy but could easily be a Sunday prayer service on the sands which was a common sight during summers of 100 years ago. The layers of concrete chalets and walkways would not be built at the foot of the cliffs until 1934.

In this 1954 scene the Victoria clock tower stands sentinel over Viking Bay. It was paid for by local MP Harry H Marks, who lived on the other side of the town at Callis Court, to celebrate Queen Victoria's diamond jubilee in 1897. It was rebuilt in 1977, the year of Queen Elizabeth's Silver Jubilee, by Thanet College students after it was badly damaged in a fire. Renovations in more recent times have been thwarted by vandals.

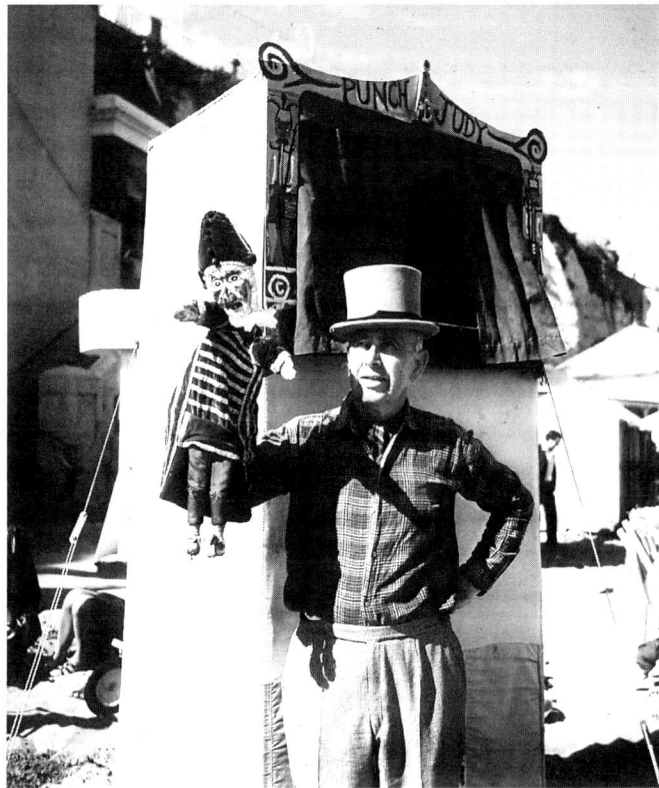

From 1962 until 1978 Peter Butchard was the Punch & Judy man at Viking and Joss Bays. Performances were given twice daily throughout the season and were preceded by a walk around the beach gathering up his young audience in Pied Piper style. By 1967, his was definitely the way to do it. Peter's out of season home was in Greenwich, to where he retired and later died, aged 100, in 2009. His distinctive wooden puppets, including a ghost and a policeman, were gifted to the National Maritime Museum.

It's enough to bring a tear to the eye! These young women would have been the dancers in the summer show at the town's Bohemia Theatre in the High Street during the 1954 season. Although they are slightly out of focus, the rarity of six girls doing the splits together on the busy sands at Viking Bay makes it special – all somewhat to the amazement of small boys close by.

Dating from at least 1952 – the year the bandstand was moved to its present location – this postcard view proves Victoria Parade has long been a popular place for parking. No doubt nearly all of the cars were British made, bearing names of a long vanished motoring era. Varying reliability meant some vehicles found it easier than others to bring their passengers for a 'stay on the coast'.

In sharp contrast to the usually busy summer scene here, this is a wintery view from 1958 looking along Victoria Parade which overlooks the main bay. A couple of hardy souls have braved the snow but are probably deciding against a walk on the beach itself – perhaps they will head to the nearby ice cream parlour for a warming drink? In the distance is the Grand Hotel and on the far left, Victoria clock tower.

One of the prime movers in starting the annual Dickens Festival Week in 1937 was Miss Gladys Waterer, seen here at the gate of Dickens House in Victoria Parade, then her home, in 1964. She filled the house with many of her hero's possessions. The house was once the home of Miss Mary Strong upon whom the author based his character Betsy Trotwood when writing David Copperfield. Following Miss Waterer's death, aged 85, in January 1971, Dickens House and its historic contents were bequested to the town's council.

The house was opened to the public as a museum during Dickens Festival Week in June 1973, the official ceremony being performed by Peter Dickens, a great grandson of the novelist. Parts of the house date from Tudor times. For some years, the house doubled as the town's tourist information office but was closed owing to spending cuts. The museum is set to reopen in 2022.

The Royal Albion Hotel started as the Phoenix but was renamed in1805 in honour of Nelson's victory at Trafalgar. One end of the hotel was where Dickens wrote part of Nicholas Nickleby in 1839 and he returned here in 1840, 1845, 1849 and 1859. This view is thought to date from 1930 but was still being used in 1950s adverts. By 1958 bed and breakfast was 25 shillings (£1.25). Today, the Albion is owned by brewer Shepherd Neame. Next door, the Omar Café was renowned for its bespoke Omar Khayyam wallpaper.

Left: Marchesi's Restaurant, which fronted Albion Street, was founded in 1886 by Swiss born Frederico Marchesi as a bakery and patisserie and evolved into one of Thanet's best known restaurants. Descendants of Frederico Marchesi, the Roger family, ran the restaurant for many years. Rightly, they prided themselves on serving high quality cuisine but decided to sell to new owners Prezzo, at the end of 2005.
Below: The restaurant's tea garden at the back of the premises, and seen from The Esplanade, was doing brisk business when this 1920s picture was captured.
Below left: The rear of Marchesi's in its final year before being sold to Prezzo.

The Esplanade, Broadstairs.

This Edwardian postcard view gives us a good indication of the length of The Esplanade. Beyond the hedge is Marchesi's Tea Garden and further away we can make out the Royal Albion Hotel and neighbouring Charles Dickens pub building. On the extreme right, a mother and her small children stop for a rest, although the little boy looks annoyed about something – perhaps he won't be able to use the beach spade he is holding after all?

Seen during the 1930s, the small gardens opposite the Balmoral Hotel in Albion Street, offered an ideal short cut to The Esplanade as well as an oasis of calm for those seeking relaxation and fresh air without venturing down to the beach. The Balmoral is thought to date from around 1850, ceasing to be a hotel by 1946. It continues to be a popular bar today.

Bathing machines line the water's edge of the main bay in this postcard image captured c1895 but there appear to be few takers for a dip in the sea, judging by the near empty sands. On the clifftop, Bleak House has yet to be extended to its present size. Beyond the bathing machines, a neat brick-walled garden juts into the sand where the Pavilion would be built nearly 40 years later.

Donkey rides on the beaches of Britain have long been an enduring part of any bucket and spade holiday – and Broadstairs' Viking Bay has been no exception. Here we see youngsters on their steeds in 1969 when the donkeys were led by Ron Saunders.

At Sunshine Coast's End – The Broadstairs Story

Arguably a defining view of Broadstairs on a busy summer's day, this scene of Viking Bay was captured at the height of holiday season in 1954 and would change little during the next three decades. On the left edge of the photo we see a popular wooden beach café which was quickly consumed in a fire caused by an electrical fault in the mid 1970s – it has never been replaced.

A complete contrast to the photo opposite is this 1958 view of a snow covered beach. Some trails of footprints confirm one or two hardy souls have ventured out but clearly didn't linger. For once, Bleak House, furthest away, lives up to its name.

Broadstairs Pavilion is the town's premier entertainment venue and was built in 1933, a few years after the council bought the Garden on the Sands upon which it stands. Pictured here in 1960, the pavilion was the summer home of Cecil Barker and his orchestra who played twice daily for many years. It's still a popular location, forming part of the Thorley Taverns portfolio.

Broadstairs Pavilion has seen a wide range of shows and concerts during its history and in recent times has been the starting point for Pilgrims Hospices charity events such as its annual Starlight Stroll – entrants are warming up here before a chilly walk in the dark in 2013 – when it's absolutely fine, if not compulsory, to wear flashing bunny ears and luminous wigs!

The York Gate was built originally in 1540 by George Culmer soon after work on the jetty was completed. The archway originally supported a portcullis and heavy gates to prevent pirates attacking the town. Lord Henniker restored the gateway in 1795 amid fears of French incursions. The traditional milk bar seen in this 1950s view, was run by the Anselmi family for more than 50 years until 2002. Further up on the left is the Palace Cinema, formerly the Windsor, which was built from a boathouse in 1911.

Top hats, frock coats and crinolines were to the fore as members of the Broadstairs Dickens Players gathered at the York Gate for a photocall to promote Dickens Festival Week in 1964. Back in the 16th century, the Culmer family granted use of the jetty and the way to it on condition it was kept 'for the good of the Commonwealth'.

The timber boat house stands at the shore end of the jetty and is thought to be at least 300 years old. The harbour master occupied the upper right hand room and has a panoramic view over the sea. From this 1964 scene, we can see that half hour sea trips cost four shillings (20p) for adults. Hercules head and whalebones have long since been moved to the left hand side of the building.

Dozens of small craft lie on the sand at low tide beside Broadstairs jetty sometime in the late 1960s. Judging by the emptiness of the beach, the picture was taken on a quiet day out of season. At this time, it was quite easy to hire a boat for a day's angling – in centuries gone by fishermen sailed as far as Iceland for cod.

Broadstairs had a succession of lifeboats between 1850 and 1912 when the RNLI closed its station. In that time three vessels were used, saving a total of 269 lives. This is the second of those lifeboats, the Christopher Waud Bradford, launching on another mission. It saw service between 1888 and 1896 and was replaced by the Francis Forbes Barton which is subject of an ongoing restoration in Ramsgate harbour. It was transported back to Kent from Boston, Lincolnshire, in 2017, where it had been rotting in a field.

An Avon Red Cat became the latest addition to the council's fleet of safety boats watching over swimmers at Broadstairs in 1969. Named Stella Maris, it was launched on 4 May by Sir Edward Heath, a year before he became Prime Minister. Here chief boatman Jim Warburton is ready for action in this 1972 view. Stella Maris, the motto on the civic town's crest, translates to Star of the Sea.

Bleak House, originally Fort House, was built in 1801 as a private residence and was extended to its present size 100 years later. It's best known as Charles Dickens' holiday home after he stayed there between 1843 and 1851. Once open to the public as a museum in the 1980s, it has become an upmarket wedding venue in more recent times. Bleak House was for sale in 2019 for £2.5 million.

Dickens Week in June has long been the annual celebration of the author's connections with the town and for many years a highlight was a costumed gathering in the gardens of Bleak House. This 1964 view shows the event in full swing. The earliest part of the building can be seen on the right and was once the home of the Fort captain, in charge of a gun battery, during the Napoleonic era.

A View on the East Cliff, Broadstairs.

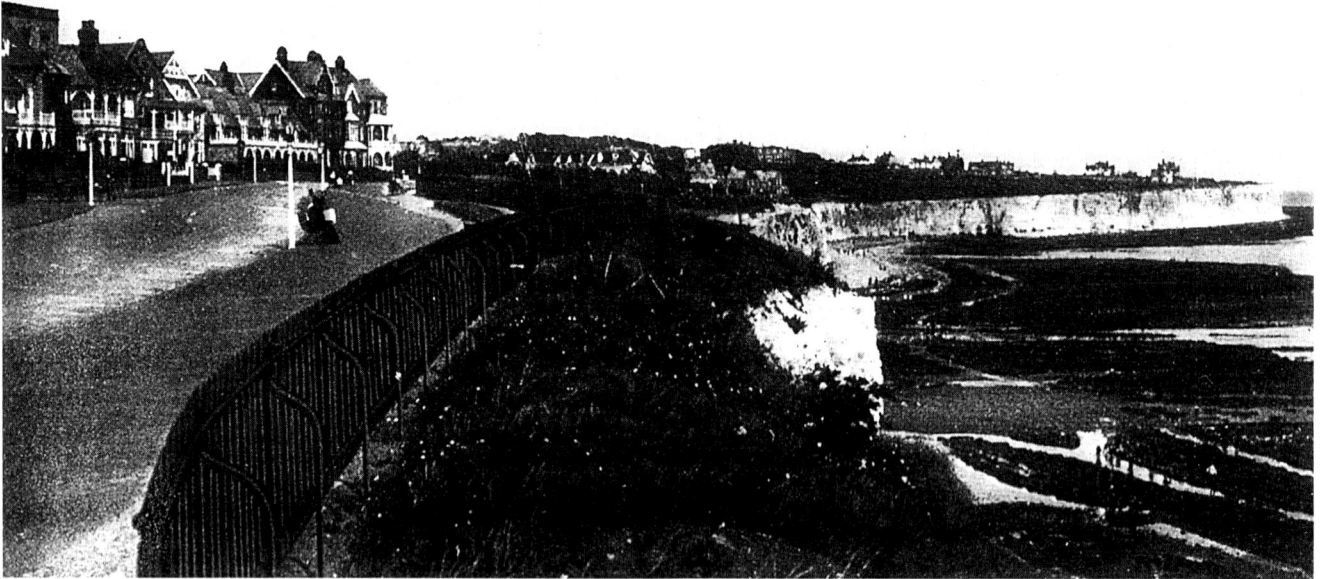

Many of the buildings fronting the East Cliff – which overlooks Stone Bay – date from when the Esplanade was built in 1894. Judging by this early 20th century view, the beach was an ideal place for hunting crabs in the many rock pools formed here. As in other parts of Thanet, a number of the larger properties along here became guest houses during the period between the two world wars.

Housing development in the 1960s and the effects of cliff erosion have changed the landscape of the East Cliff. The beach is far sandier today while access to it has been made easier with a twisting slope down. Here, the promenade is being built in 1970 at a cost of £350,000, much of it paid from government grants.

The Broadstairs Viking invasion of 1949

For decades a symbol of Thanet, a subject of postcards contrasting it with 1960s channel-crossing hovercraft and, more recently, the centre piece of a cycle trail, the Viking ship sitting atop cliffs at Pegwell Bay, a few miles from Broadstairs, makes for a majestic sight. But how many of us have considered how and why it got there?

Were such a venture to be tried today, it would be worthy of a six part reality TV series, backed with 24/7 social media updates, recording the highs and lows of its crew as it made a perilous 1,000 mile journey across the North Sea.

Back in July 1949 that was exactly what happened – minus onboard video and social media, of course.

Wearing winged helmets and authentic dress, a contingent of 50 Vikings sailed from Esbjerg in Denmark aboard the replica sailing ship Hugin to land at Broadstairs main bay on 28 July 1949.

The Hugin, as the ship was named, sailed from Denmark with 50 bearded men aboard living as their predecessors did, to celebrate the 1,500th anniversary of the Viking Jute invasion of Kent by Hengist and Horsa in 449.

The ship's arrival made big news around the world and some 30,000 people packed every available standpoint in Broadstairs to see it land on the main beach – ever since known as Viking Bay in honour of the occasion.

From early morning on Thursday 28 July – at the height of the holiday season – trains emptied excited visitors on both platforms of Broadstairs station.

Cars and coaches appeared from nowhere. It was then exceptional to see side roads and car parks jammed bumper to bumper. Some cafés had stayed open all night before while hawkers did a roaring trade selling telescopes.

Everyone was waiting for 2pm, the hour Hugin would sail on the high tide into the bay. The vessel was in sight from quite early on having arrived by the North Goodwin lightship ready for a launch to escort her for the last lap of the journey.

It was the sunny day everyone had hoped for – not least the local council which had been a driving force of the whole project. Crowds flocked to the seafront and jetty while many more packed local restaurants and cafés from mid morning.

Policemen patrolling the streets had been told to keep traffic flowing and sightseers happy. For the first time in Thanet they were using walkie-talkie radio, albeit bulky back packs.

Although the original invasion had taken place at Pegwell Bay in 449, the story goes that Broadstairs was chosen for the re-enactment because the Chairman of that town's publicity committee, Cllr BJ Pearson, had made quite sure its subscription to the Travel Association, which laid on the event, was fully paid up. Apparently, neighbouring Ramsgate's was not!

Long before the appointed hour, Broadstairs seafront was packed six deep. The knoll at the bandstand end of the bay was invisible while at the other, the Elizabethan jetty was almost sinking into the harbour there were so many people. The beach itself was simply swarming with

Around 30,000 people crowded the beach, renamed Viking Bay in honour of the occasion, to see the Hugin land. Every likely vantage point was taken to ensure a good view.

As spear carrying Vikings make their way up the beach, the only fight was getting through the crowds, roared the Daily Graphic in its news coverage of the occasion.

This time though it was a flag-waving holiday army which greeted the latter day invaders. Their progress was hindered slightly by an off shore breeze which made the sail useless, so the crew had to use its oars. A strong sun glinted on to dipping blades and the helmets of the bronzed Vikings added life to an already colourful scene.

Hugin swept on to the shore only 15 minutes behind time and as it did so hundreds pushed forward to take photos or get a better view, engulfing press and VIPs.

Besieged by the scrumming crowd, the Norsemen waved spears above their heads in acknowledgement as they climbed out of the ship. Their chief, a tall Dane named Erik Suell Kiersgaard, led his crew on to the sands to be welcomed by Prince Georg of Denmark, with the Chairman of the council and the Archbishop of Canterbury, Dr Geoffrey Fisher. A bunch of roughly dressed Anglo-Saxons were on hand to offer the crew a tribal pot of mead.

The carnival atmosphere was electric. There was a civic banquet at the nearby Grand Hotel that evening, followed by a public fireworks display on the jetty.

sightseers and a posse of film cameramen, photographers and reporters waited on the water's edge as a silver band played in an enclosure.

As the outline of the ship appearing on the skyline enlarged into the ship's sleek hull, the air of expectancy grew tenfold.

From its raven standard to its painted shields, the Hugin confirmed the fear that ancient Viking vessels must have struck into the lightly armed fifth century Britons.

The following day the ship was rowed round to Ramsgate and at Cliffsend 10,000 watched a re-enactment of the original landing itself. Here, a British camp had been built and during the pageant King Vortigern exchanged his kingdom for the hand of Hengist's daughter Rowena. Later, Prince Georg unveiled a tablet on the site. Another formal reception followed in Ramsgate that evening.

The Hugin's crew was feted across Thanet by the three local councils of the day, each providing a civic dinner in their honour – as these menues testify.

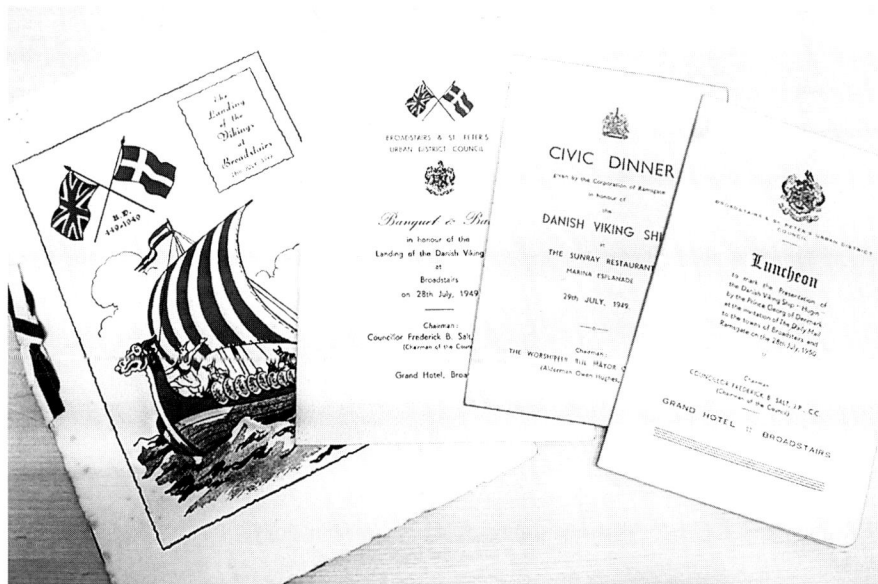

Hugin took to the water once again with her crew to sail around the coast to Margate for a third civic reception. This time 40,000 turned out to see the ship arrive in the old harbour.

It was announced after the Thanet landings the Daily Mail had purchased the Hugin and would be presenting it jointly to Broadstairs and Ramsgate – somewhat to Margate's annoyance – once it had completed a tour taking in London and a number of British seaside resorts.

Almost a year later Prince Georg returned to these shores for the formal handover of the ship at its Pegwell Bay site with Thanet leaders united in goodwill for the event.

A souvenir programme of the Broadstairs landing notes the Hugin was built as closely as possible to an original in 10 weeks by craftsmen at Frederikssund near Copenhagen. Its design is based on Viking ships used between the fifth and ninth centuries. The vessel is nearly 80 feet long, 40 feet high to the masthead and weighs about 15 tons. It was launched on 1 July 1949 by the wife of the then Prime Minister of Denmark, Mrs Hedtoft. In Nordic legend Hugin was a black raven sent to earth by the god Odin to report on the affairs of man.

At Sunshine Coast's End – The Broadstairs Story

Its crew was drawn from hundreds of volunteer applicants, aged between 19 and 24, all members of the country's rowing associations. Aside from putting on Viking clothing for the voyage, growing a beard was a requirement of the job.

The skipper and navigator Captain Jensen, was equipped only with a sextant for navigation. It's a fair bet though the modern warship escort would have helped out with direction finding if necessary!

Hugin set sail from Esbjerg, the west coast port of Jutland, with the crew taking turns at the oars in teams of 16. During their crossing they lived as Vikings of old. No smoking or drinking was allowed, save only for what the barrels provided. Sleep was snatched on the hard benches and boards while simple meals were cooked over a fire on a metal plate. Shelter was in a tent amidships. By the time they arrived these Danes had settled down to some hard living, made rougher for having to weather a storm on the way which saw them put into port for a while in Holland.

Erik Thrane, then only 19 years old and the second youngest aboard, kept a log for the Daily Graphic newspaper which it collected from him when Hugin was anchored off the Goodwins.

During the ship's sea trials he noted that everywhere they went in Denmark, parties were given in their honour. One night he missed the launch back to Hugin and had to swim out to it.

Despite choppy seas, the crew managed to enjoy a hearty sing-song while waiting near the North Goodwin lightship before their landing on the beach at Broadstairs.

Four days into the voyage, the seas became higher and almost everyone on board was ill while wind and driving rain hampered their efforts. Several people fell off their benches while trying to sleep as the ship heeled and rolled. Erik was terribly seasick and couldn't hold down a glass of water, he said. Later the captain ordered sufferers to gargle on beer.

The weather turned and it became blistering hot as Hugin, nearing England, managed a steady six knots in the calmer waters. A canvas shelter was erected on deck to provide welcome shade.

The publicity value to Broadstairs was inestimable. The ship's arrival featured in both Movietone and Gaumont cinema newsreels, BBC radio broadcasts around the world and international coverage via major news agencies – print and cinematic – at home and abroad. One agency reported it had 'never known a story to go down so well'.

Long after all the furore had died down and the 'invaders' were wintering in Denmark, rumour had it there was another story of that July day. Had a certain councillor's wife run off with the Viking chief?

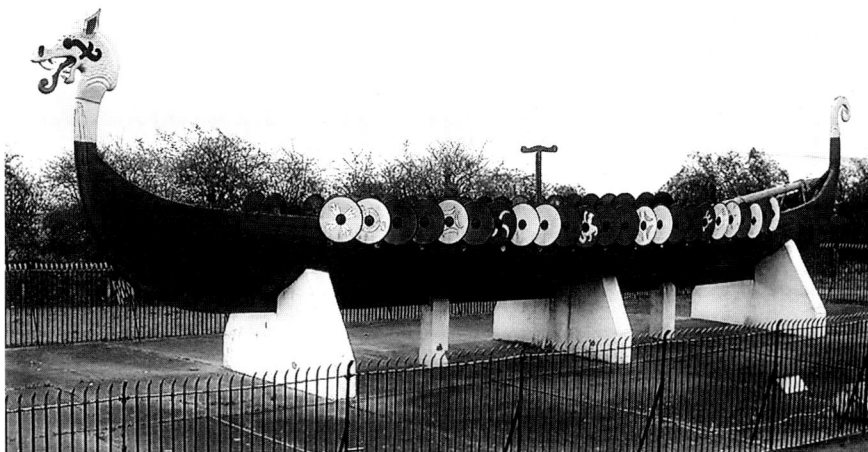

The Hugin, seen here prior to its extensive 2005 restoration, has been a popular Thanet landmark atop the cliffs of Pegwell Bay for more than 70 years.

• The Daily Graphic gave extensive coverage of the Broadstairs invasion with pictures on the front, back and centre pages. The Viking ship though was in complete contrast to another form of transport which was just making its tentative debut at the time. The same issue of the newspaper reported that the world's first jet engined airliner, the De Havilland Comet, had successfully climbed to 8,000 feet on its maiden test flight from Hatfield during a 31 minute flight.

Tragic shooting spree ended at Stone Bay

For much of the 1950s there was a small piece of America in Thanet. RAF Manston had been taken over by the US Air Force as a forward base when the cold war started to warm up. During their eight year long presence the Americans made their impression on the local area in many different ways – much of it positive. Tragically, one made his own mark in the most deadly fashion.

In August 1955 Airman Second Class Napoleon Green, 21, from the tough south side of Chicago, was due to face a court martial alleging he stole a wallet containing US$120.

The night before his appearance he told the men in his barrack hut he was going to 'get' his enemies – the air force police who had grilled him.

"I got a list here," he warned. "On it are the names of the guys I'm out to get." The other men simply laughed.

Next morning, Green was up for 6am reveille dressed in olive denims and baseball cap. After breakfast he returned to the barracks and made

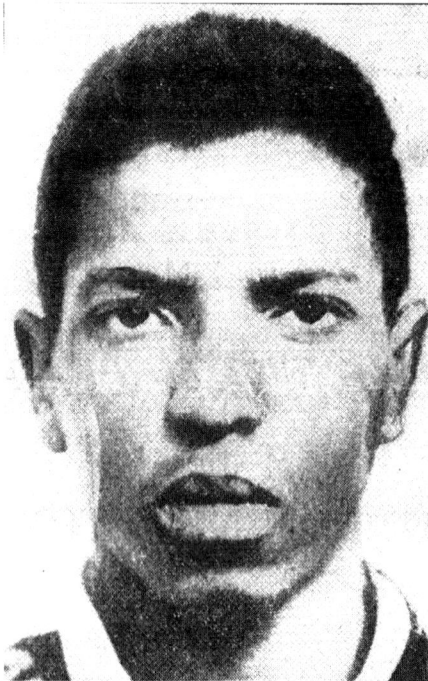

Far left: 21 year old Napoleon Green, a US serviceman based at Manston who, left, armed with stolen pistol and rifle killed three people and wounded nine others before shooting himself on the beach at Stone Bay in August 1955.

another threat: "If you guys are not out of here in 10 minutes, when I come back, I'm going to start shooting."

Soon after 9am Green broke off his work in a supply room and walked across the camp. Minutes later he was in the armoury and had started annoying the section clerk.

Airman Third Class James Hall, working there alone, told him to get behind the counter – where people usually drew their equipment. But Green went over to a stencil machine and started banging it.

Hall told him to quit before he broke it. He hit it another four or five times then walked to the edge of the counter. Hall then heard what sounded like the click of a gun being cocked.

He said later: "It was then I realised he had a gun. Neither of us said a word during this time. Green turned to the gun cage and hit the lock with a hatchet."

He was now pointing a .45 calibre automatic pistol in Hall's direction. Hall tried to get out of the room by saying he would get the cage keys. Green told him to stay put.

"Then he smashed the lock and got the ammunition. As he scooped a handful, he still kept the gun pointing at my body."

Green helped himself to a semi-automatic rifle and left with it in one hand and the pistol in the other. He was about to give Manston a trail of death and horror.

Right: The shootings made national and international headlines – this is how the Daily Sketch reported the drama.

DAILY SKETCH [2d]

BEACH GUN BATTLE

AMAZING PICTURES

The Sketch was there

GUNMAN BEHIND THIS ROCK

ARMED U.S. AIR POLICE MOVE IN

MOBILE POLICEMAN

UNARMED BRITISH POLICE

The shooting drama is nearly over. Behind a rock at the water's edge crouches a coloured American airman . . . armed U.S. Air Police move in. Seconds later he is in their sights desperately pressing . . . his rifle trigger.

By PETER STEWART, Broadstairs, Kent, Wednesday

NAPOLEON GREEN, 21-year-old Negro from Chicago, ran amok to-day, shot to death three men, wounded nine others. Then he was killed in a gun battle on a holiday beach.

He did it because he was due to be court martialled at Manston air station for stealing a wallet containing £10.

Green denied the theft—in Chicago style—made a hate list of the police who questioned him.

To-day, in Chicago gangster tradition, he went after the man at the top of the hate list.

But Napoleon never got him. The man had gone to the camp laundry.

Instead the quiet little coloured U.S. Air Force supplies clerk armed himself with a stolen automatic, shot dead two U.S. policemen, an R.A.F. corporal, and

Back Page

THE KILLER

The crazed gunman—U.S. airman Napoleon Green. He shot three people dead and wounded nine others.

FERGUSON SETS A NEW STANDARD IN TELEVALUE

FERGUSON's

He returned to his barrack hut where many of the men were off duty or about to go to sleep.

Nobody took any notice until Green fired his first shot straight into the stomach of another 21 year old, Nelson Gresham. A friend of Green, he had told him to put the gun down before someone got hurt.

Gresham fell to the floor, to die from his wounds three hours later. The others in the hut dived for cover through doors and windows. Shouting rent the air.

The gunman strolled calmly out of the quarters and fired on a nearby group of men, wounding Airman Second Class Quannah F Parker in the hand.

The noise had brought men rushing to the doors of Hut 846, the squadron's admin office building. Here Green shot and seriously wounded Airman Lester Hunt in the chest and grazed Master Sergeant John Gouviea in the mouth.

RAF policeman Corporal Raymond Grayer wasn't so lucky. Oblivious to the drama unfolding, he was riding past on his bicycle when he was killed in a hail of bullets.

Master Sergeant Lawrence Valesquez left behind a wife and four young children when he was killed at point blank range by Napoleon Green.

Still shooting his way down the base main road, Green gunned down Master Sergeant Lawrence Valesquez. The 33 year old father of four fell dead with a bullet in his brain. At the same time 18 year old British typist Wendy Welton was hit on the hip.

The killer moved towards the main gate, firing at an air policeman there, and sending a burst through the side of a car bringing people to work. Inside, driver Leonard Broadbent was unhurt but passengers Ann Cockburn and Ian Yeomans were injured.

Before leaving the camp Green wounded three more civilian staff. On the road outside Green came upon control tower NCO, Master Sgt Rowley McDaniels, getting into his beige Ford Popular. Green thrust the pistol through the car window, shouting for him to open the door.

"I leaned over and he got in the back seat," McDaniels said later. "He was sticking the .45 in the back of my head. He said 'Drive, mister, drive'. I'm an obliging sort of man when someone has a .45.

"I asked him where he wanted to go and he said Margate. I told him I didn't know the way and he would have to tell me. We got to a road junction and I asked him 'which way?' He said: 'Down there, that road'.

"When we got to an intersection I asked him: 'Why don't you just take the car? I'll walk back to the base'. He said he couldn't drive a British car.

"I said: 'I'll gladly teach you boy. It'll only take a minute. It's very simple – just like any other car'.

"We pulled up and he ordered me out. I walked away without looking back until I heard him drive off. Then I got a lift in a butcher's truck and went to Margate police station."

Green drove on to Broadstairs and down the narrow main street. Eventually he reached the jetty opposite the Tartar Frigate public house.

Despite being armed and dangerous, Napoleon Green was told 'you can't park here', by 70 year old attendant Fred Beecham when he drove up to Broadstairs jetty.

Fred Beecham, a 70 year old car park attendant saw the car draw up: "A man jumped out and left the engine running," he said. "I told him he couldn't park there and he replied 'If they want me they must come and get me.'" Green ran down the slope to the sands and disappeared.

The attendant's impression was this was all part of some Army manoeuvre but he did tell harbour master Arthur Pay who removed the car key and called the police.

By now the word was well and truly out that there was a crazed gunman on the loose. American Air Police were quickly joined by RAF redcaps and civilian police. The hunt was on – and the well armed Americans were in no mood for compromise.

As Green, still carrying rifle and pistol, ran along the beach, hundreds of holidaymakers were in his path. It was a typical height of the holiday season scene with parents in deck chairs, children building sandcastles and others enjoying a dip in the sea.

Some gazed curiously at this troubled figure. "I thought he must be on some kind of military exercise," said one man. "I reckoned he was going to shoot seagulls," said another. "I thought it was a film stunt," said a delivery boy.

After a while Green reached Stone Bay, a rocky beach to the west of the main Broadstairs Viking Bay.

Green's pursuers were closing in fast. While some officers warned people to stay clear as they chased him across the beach, others were heading him off by running down the cliff steps of North Foreland Estate. Further along the coast, the beach at Joss Bay was hurriedly cleared. The final showdown was set. The olive green figures of US policemen and six local

Local police and USAF personnel escort holidaymakers off the beach to safety using the '39 Steps' flight of stairs cut into the cliff on the North Foreland Estate.

constables moved as one towards the rocks. The tide was out but Green's uniform gave him some temporary camouflage as he lay quiet. Then he was seen through binoculars from the clifftops and his position shouted to the men below.

Those on the clifftop held their breath. As they did, the silence was broken by a volley of shots from Green. Fire was returned and Green was hit. He fell in a small pool writhing. Underneath him was his rifle. More shots followed as Green, who had killed three and wounded nine in 90 minutes, fired two more bullets into his own chest.

Seconds later an American crawled on to the rock and looked down. The pool was now crimson. He raised a hand. "OK fellas," he shouted, "he's dead." The battle was over.

Not surprisingly, the story was big news around the world and looking at some of those cuttings now, it's interesting to reflect on how the British media, at least, handled it. 'Crazed gunman on loose', 'Gun battle drama on holiday beach' 'Mad killer lies dead' and

End of the trail of blood and terror

It's all over, local police and armed servicemen take a breather. In the ambulance is the body of Napoleon Green.

'Camp killer: I will die' were among the louder headlines and were backed up by pictures of gun toting Yanks on the beach and clifftop. Hopefully, the operation would have been handled with greater care and precision today if it were to be repeated – certainly it would be comforting to think tourists gathering to watch would have been kept much further away from the action.

A walk through the centre of town

A tranquil moment as long skirted ladies process down the High Street, perhaps on their way to the beach, in this view dating from c1905 before the intervention of the car. The road turning away to the left is Charlotte Street. In the foreground, a tearoom is accessed by walking through the confectioner's. The adjoining building, facing the High Street, opened as a new Tesco store in July 2021.

Value, civility and satisfaction were the watchwords of draper William Evans, grandfather of the author, at 3 Charlotte Street, who traded in Broadstairs for 25 years. Household linens, blankets, towels, summer dresses and beach wear were sold in abundance when this view was taken in 1955. William died a year later and the business was sold to Jack and Marjorie Park who ran it until the mid 1970s. The premises were then taken over by Blackburn's to sell soft furnishings. The shop is home to a boutique today.

Arguably the most picturesque part of the centre of Broadstairs is Serene Place, just off the High Street at the bottom of the hill. In 1967 two shops were located here. Formerly the Lancaster House tea room, Joyce sold hats while neighbouring Victoriana sold antiques and china. Castle House at the far end was the home of old time music hall star Ted Gatty. He was the man who gave Danny La Rue his name. These days there is no trace of the two shops having existed. The bay windowed frontages have been removed from 16th century Serene House but it is recognised as an historic building of Kent, bearing a diamond shaped plaque above the front door. The setting is as attractive as ever.
• Note the council poster at the bottom right of the photo warning owners they would be fined £5 if their dogs fouled the footways.

8706. High Street, Broadstairs.

A prestigious Alvis is the only vehicle in this 1932 scene looking down the High Street. John T May, whose office is on the left, was a local builder and it was for this firm that the father of Prime Minister Sir Edward Heath worked as a carpenter before starting his own business at Kingsgate. There has since been considerable rebuilding of what is now the Nationwide Building Society on the right as both it and the adjoining property have each lost a storey. Just out of view on this side, an old cinema, remembered for its sliding roof, was demolished in the 1950s, later to become Woolworth's and Tesco's. The builder's office is a charity shop.

The Bohemia Theatre traces its origins from 1905 when a concert party called the Broadstairs Bohemians performed here. Then, the site was known as The Lawn but such was its success, it was renamed The Bohemia and the theatre was built in 1922. The Bohemia burnt down in November 1963 after becoming derelict but was in good order when this view was taken in June 1960. Note the name of Jack Warner, of Dixon of Dock Green fame, on the concert billboards. He had a home at Kingsgate for many years.

Slightly further up the hill that is the High Street, this view dates from 1905. On the extreme left is the Providence Strict Baptist Chapel, marked by an ornamental lamp. The flint buildings towards the bottom of the hill were knocked down in the 1950s to widen the road. Inset: The demolition work in progress while beyond that lies Woolworth's store in the block of modern shops.

At the bottom of Vere Road, backing on to houses and a coach & car park are the town's allotments. Having the chance to grow your own food has been important to people for many years and in 1960, the allotments looked well tended. The houses in the background are along Bradstow Way and Crow Hill.

The War Memorial,
Broadstairs

Standing outside one of the entrances to Pierremont Hall is the town's war memorial. This was dedicated on 16 June 1923 by archdeacon Ven LJ White-Thompson. It had taken £1,000 and five years of vigorous discussion on where to site the Portland Stone memorial before it was finally unveiled. The council was only able to carry out the work when the lease on Pierremont Hall was bought in 1922 for £5,500 by a syndicate of four notable citizens, frustrated at the lack of progress on building the memorial.

Summer rides around Thanet on East Kent's fleet of cream and red open top buses were a highlight for many and have been reintroduced by today's operator Stagecoach in recent times, albeit on a shorter route. In this late 1960s scene, a converted wartime built Guy utility bus has just trundled up the hill of the High Street, passing Arter & Co's garage on the other side of the road, as it gradually heads to Minnis Bay near Birchington, via Cliftonville and Margate. The garage changed hands a couple of times between the 1970s and the early 2000s before being knocked down and replaced by a Co-op convenience store with flats above.

9971. Pierremont House & Park, Broadstairs.

Built in 1785 as a private residence for Thomas Forsyth, Pierremont Hall is now open to the community for public and private events under the ownership of the town council. The building is Grade II Listed and has been extensively renovated in recent times. The Duchess of Kent and a young Princess Victoria holidayed at Pierremont from 1826 to 1836 while by 1896 it had been sold to Leonard Posnett who used it as a school. Most of the original 30 acres of land were developed as housing and the building and remaining park were sold to the urban district council in 1927 who used it as its offices and chamber until Thanet District Council was created in April 1974. In more recent times, part of it has been the home of Thanet's driving test centre.

Set opposite the main driveway up to the railway station was the Railway Tavern, a handy place for weary travellers to rest after getting off the train. The London, Chatham and Dover Railway reached Broadstairs in 1863 bringing people to the town in less than two hours from London for the first time. The pub is called Crampton's these days, named after Thomas Crampton, the railway engineer born in Broadstairs. It is part of the Thorley Taverns chain whose headquarters is in the town's former police station in Gladstone Road.

Broadstairs Station.

A young boy wearing a school cap turns to eye the camera as this 1930s picture is captured. He and his father are walking up the slope towards the Ramsgate bound, or down side, of the railway station. On the other side of the track there used to be extensive sidings but today the library and a car park have long taken their place. Until the 1970s, when a footbridge was built over both tracks, passengers had to walk under the roadbridge, to the left of this photo, to reach the other side for trains to Margate and beyond.

The railway bridge, seen left, was rebuilt in May 1901 to provide more headroom for passengers riding on the top deck of trams. Perhaps because of the bridge, shopkeepers on the nearby Broadway regarded themselves as slightly separate from the rest of the High Street and were happy to band into their own traders' association. At this time, the town's main Post Office was on the far end of the row at the junction with Grosvenor Road. Beyond the Post Office, but out of sight, lies Crampton Tower.

The Broadstairs & St Peter's Mail was the town's local paper from 1903 until 1979 and owned by Ramsgate's East Kent Times. The Mail was named in tribute to Lord Northcliffe, founder of the Daily Mail who lived at Reading Street. The town's paper moved to 13 The Broadway in 1910 when its editor was Amos Hickmore. The premises have been a barber's shop for many years.

Thornton Wilder's comedy play The Skin Of Our Teeth, no doubt produced by one of Broadstairs local amateur drama groups, is getting some mobile publicity around town ahead of performances at the Memorial Hall, sometime during the late 1950s or early 1960s. The view also captures well one part of the Broadway Garage with its line of Shell petrol pumps and workshop.

Captured during the early 1960s, Broadway Garage occupied – and still does so – the corner of Park Road, seen on the right hand side and St Peter's Road on the left, and facing the Broadway itself. An Austin dealer when photographed, the garage later sold Volkswagens as JC Morrison. There are no longer any car sales but the premises form a busy petrol station and mini-supermarket.

Broadstairs son's road to Number 10

Politics is a cruel way of life – even, or especially, some might say, for those who make it to the very top of the tree. One minute you have the country's support and the next, you can be a total pariah.

After stepping down from that lofty platform, history is not always kind enough to record your successes and you can be swiftly forgotten.

Ted Heath was born in the ground floor flat of this house, 1 Holmwood Villas, Albion Road, St Peter's, on 9 July 1916.

Unless you were around in the early 1970s, there's a chance you might not have heard of, or readily recall, Sir Edward Heath, Britain's Conservative Prime Minister from June 1970 to March 1974.

Best remembered now for taking Britain into the Common Market, introducing a three day working week during a bitter coal miners' strike, accompanied by power cuts, and battling rising inflation, he is Broadstairs most famous son.

Unlike many of today's politicians, Edward – or Ted to all who knew him – was born to working class parents. His father, William, was a carpenter and his mother, Edith, a housemaid. There was no silver spoon for Ted, meaning he had to work hard to get through grammar school and on to university before war intervened. He was an MP for half a century and retired from Westminster life as a millionaire.

Ted was born in a ground floor flat at 1 Holmwood Villas, in Albion Road, St Peter's, on Sunday 9 July 1916. An air raid was in progress at the time.

He was still a babe-in-arms when his parents moved to Crayford where his father had a wartime job with the Vickers aircraft company. They did not return to Broadstairs until 1923, moving to a three bed semi in King Edward Avenue. By then Ted was seven years old and started attending St Peter's church elementary school.

Ted Heath was seven years old when he first attended the village school in Flint Grove, St Peter's, pictured here in 1970. The building ceased to be a school in 1998.

"Ted was a little bigger than other boys of his age. His mother always sent him to school impeccably dressed, a condition he managed to maintain all day, which helped make him a model pupil.

"When he was 11 years old he passed a scholarship to Chatham House Grammar School, Ramsgate, which nobody ever doubted he would."

By then, one facet of Ted's personality was beginning to show. It would bother writers and political commentators during the decades to follow, especially once he became leader of the Conservative party. It was his air of detachment.

Even Ted's friends around Broadstairs could not agree on the precise word for it. Shy, aloof, reserved, lonely – all were used to qualify their admiration for him.

Part of his character that showed at Chatham House was his strict sense of discipline. The other boys soon learned not to fall foul of prefect Heath. One lad recalled taking 10 minutes too long to change back into uniform after games – and got six of the best with a gym shoe for his tardiness.

Years later his assistant head teacher, James Bird, remembered Ted's abilities: "He soon proved to be a good all-rounder, at times brilliant. He was better academically – especially in history and maths – than in practical subjects, though he tried hard to do things with his hands.

In 1935, Ted won a scholarship to Baliol College, Oxford, to read politics, philosophy and economics. It was while there he further developed his love of music – he was already an accomplished organist and conductor. During this pre-war era Ted visited Germany and saw first hand the horrors wrought upon that country by the Nazi party, avowing him to work for a united Europe. When war did follow, Ted joined the Royal Artillery, rising to become a Lieutenant Colonel before briefly joining the Civil Service.

In 1950, he was elected as the MP for Bexley, a seat he would hold for his entire political career, stepping down in 2001, as Father of The House, the title given to the Commons' longest serving member.

Ted became leader of the Conservatives in 1965, its first to have been voted into the role, rather than to have 'emerged'. He saw off competition from other political heavyweights Enoch Powell and Reginald Maudling. Thus began his long rivalry with Labour Prime Minster Harold Wilson.

Ted's growing political workload did not deter him from continuing to be a regular visitor to Broadstairs, spending weekends with his father and step-mother Mary (William remarried after Edith died from cancer during the 1950s) at their home near Dumpton Gap. Ted would enjoy catching up with friends at the Tartar Frigate pub and sailing with the town's yacht club.

For Ted, sailing would prove to be a vital antidote to the political cut and thrust of Westminster – yet it was a hobby he only took up in 1966, when he was 50 years old. He had been taught to sail by local school teacher

Sailing became a passion in middle age for Ted Heath, seen here in the late 1960s with friend Rex Walden off Broadstairs, probably aboard Ted's boat Blue Heather.

Steady as you go! A local signwriter is caught midway through his task of painting the name Blue Heather on the sides of Ted Heath's boat in the late 1960s.

The Heath family returned to Broadstairs in 1923, moving to this three bedroom semi-detached house named Helmdon at 4 King Edward Avenue, seen here in 1970.

Gordon Knight. Their first lesson was held in a force six gale and both got a good soaking. "The boat was about a third full of water, but Ted had no fears," he said afterwards.

Fellow members of Broadstairs Sailing Club regarded Ted, the man in the blue sweater, as an asset if not a spectacular sailor and admired his determination at taking to the sea in comparative middle age.

In the late 1960s, Ted owned both a speedboat and a Fireball class dinghy which were kept at the harbour during the week and came out whenever circumstances allowed.

In December 1968, Denis Pitts, a Sunday Times magazine reporter, trailed Ted during one of his weekend breaks which took in a Sunday morning visit to the Tartar Frigate.

He noted: "The locals gave little sign of deference or diffidence. They were obviously used to having him there."

Ted told him: "You know, a lot of people think there is something phoney about my going into pubs and talking to people. It isn't phoney. I went to school with a lot of these people. I've known them all my life."

Above: Celebrating election success – and becoming Prime Minister – with family and friends at his parents' home in Dumpton Gap Road in late June 1970.

Right: Ted Heath conducting during one of his famous Broadstairs Christmas carol concerts held at the Grand Ballroom.

The following year Ted's skills as a helmsman had clearly developed as he would sail his ocean-going yacht Morning Cloud II to victory in the tough Sydney-Hobart race off Australia. He would also captain Britain's Admiral's Cup winning team in 1971, the only time a serving Prime Minister has won a major international sporting trophy.

A highlight of the Broadstairs social calendar from 1936 until the late 1970s were the Christmas carol concerts at the Grand Ballroom. Ted had established the charity events when still a teenager and maintained the tradition during his Prime Ministerial years. By then, the concerts had become a major scrum as the world's media jockeyed for position for a photo of Ted conducting the choir!

Throughout his life, Ted remained a single man. We have already said he was perhaps shy and reserved but it appears there was at least one woman who saw past those traits. At some time in the 1930s, Ted was knocked off his bicycle in Broadstairs and taken to the surgery of local GP Dr Raven to check for injuries. While there, Ted bumped into his daughter Kay and an enduring friendship began.

They wrote to each other throughout the Second World War and despite working in different parts of the country afterwards, kept up their friendship.

However, by 1950, and perhaps realising Ted's new political career would always come first, Kay had tired of waiting for Ted to propose marriage and had met someone else. Her choice made a lasting impact upon him and he never looked at another woman.

After losing two elections in 1974, Ted held on to party leadership for another year, eventually being toppled by Margaret Thatcher. He would become one of her most bitter critics, some calling this 'Ted's 20 year long sulk'. Salt would be added to the wounds later when Mrs Thatcher slapped VAT on yachts – 'my retirement is ruined', lamented Ted to his friends.

He died in 2005, aged 89, at his home Arundells, which is set within the bounds of Salisbury Cathedral, and is open to the public.

Above: The Heath family moved to their detached house in Dumpton Gap Road during 1966, taking the Helmdon name with them. The house is seen here four years later. A bedroom was decorated for Ted to use during his regular weekend visits, both as PM and opposition leader. Below: Completely built on now, cornfields opposite the house offered a pleasant view at the time.

Eyewitness to an air crash in St Peter's

The vicar of St Peter's, Reverend Laurens Sargent, had just realised he had let his weekly sermon go on rather too long, perhaps by as much as 10 minutes, but he and his congregation would very quickly be extremely glad that he had.

The last few minutes of that service on Sunday 27 April 1952 were apprehensive ones to say the least for there had been a deafening explosion nearby which reminded many of a wartime air raid. Not surprisingly, most people had lost concentration for the final hymn of the service.

What those 300 or so worshippers did not know until they streamed out of the church was that an American Air Force Thunderjet fighter had crash-landed in St Peter's High Street, little more than 100 yards away.

Seconds earlier, local newspaper reporter Bill Evans, enjoying a Sunday morning walk along the clifftop at Dumpton Gap on the other side of town, was alerted by a frightening sight.

A stricken American jet fighter crashed on this spot in April 1952. Those killed are remembered by a plaque on the corner of St Peter's High Street with Ranelagh Grove. The parish church can just be seen in the background.

In the early 1950s people on the Thanet towns were used to seeing USAF aircraft flying above the isle, for they were based at Manston. But this aircraft, with others streaking across the sky just inland from the coast, was clearly in trouble as flames and smoke were pouring from it while rapidly losing height. As it went out of sight behind the built up part of Broadstairs, there was a distant bump – followed by an eerie silence.

Bill had already turned back for home, running nearly a mile to get home and to his car. Once driving, he wasn't quite sure where he was going but after turning a few corners he found a trail of smoke rising from the St Peter's direction. Police and fire brigade had just arrived as he got there. The plane had crashed on the sub-branch of the village bank and an adjoining ironmonger's shop, reducing a flat to rubble and wrecking three neighbouring houses.

There was time for Bill to phone the Press Association, the national news agency, to let them know of the crash before piecing the story together.

An American Thunderjet, similar to the one that crashed in St Peter's one Sunday morning in 1952, refuels in mid-air – the first aircraft to be able to do so.

Back at the church, the vicar was saying: "Had I finished my sermon promptly, more than 300 people would have been walking along the High Street when the plane crashed. Many would have been waiting at the bus stop near the bank."

It transpired that, as the final hymn was being sung, a few people had left church early and had reached the end of its path joining the road as the plane exploded less than another minute's walk away.

Many of the windows in the high street were shattered by the blast and, as firemen tackled the flames, woodwork crackled on properties across the street. Burning fuel showered the vicinity while 1,000 rounds of ammunition exploded. Blazing paraffin, stored in the ironmonger's, soon set light to other properties.

As the aircraft plunged through the bank and shop, making a deep crater in a garden, the pilot, Captain Clifford Fogarty, 29, from New York, was catapulted some 30 feet to his death.

It took more than six hours for rescue workers to find the bodies of the 70 year old ironmonger William Read and his wife Evelyn, buried 15 feet beneath the ruins of their shop. Three other people were burned and injured, including an eight year old boy who had been feeding rabbits in his garden. One of the adults, Ellen Collier, later died of her injuries.

It was revealed later that shortly after taking off from Manston with three other planes on a training flight, Clifford and his plane were quickly in difficulty. Airborne for only 45 seconds in a finger four formation, his number three in the pattern radioed Clifford to say his port wing was alight. Clifford's commanding officer, flying one of the other craft, immediately ordered him to 'land in the first flat space you see'.

Part of the scene of devastation in St Peter's High Street some hours after the crash. A crowd has formed while rescuers work to find bodies and clear wreckage of the plane.

Clifford turned inland over Ramsgate in that search and then above Dumpton – where he was seen by Bill – before his plane started exploding over Broadstairs, by which time he had lost control and, seconds later, crashed.

One of his colleagues said afterwards: "We had reached between 800 and 1,000 feet when I saw his plane blazing. We had enough air speed for Cliff to have used his ejector seat and parachute to safety. He could have used it and got away with his life, but he obviously stayed with the plane and tried to clear the town."

Clifford left a wife and child who lived with him in Margate. His body was returned to New York for burial.

In 2002, half a century after the tragedy, a memorial stone was laid at the spot in St Peter's remembering all four of the people who died.

A stroll around St Peter's & Reading Street

37044. VICARAGE STREET, ST. PETER'S BROADSTAIRS.

Bereft of cars, Vicarage Street was a peaceful place when this view was taken in the 1930s. On the right, halfway up is the entrance to Oaklands Court. Vicarage Street was known as St Peter's Street in the 1861 census but had swopped to its former name when the next one was taken 10 years after.

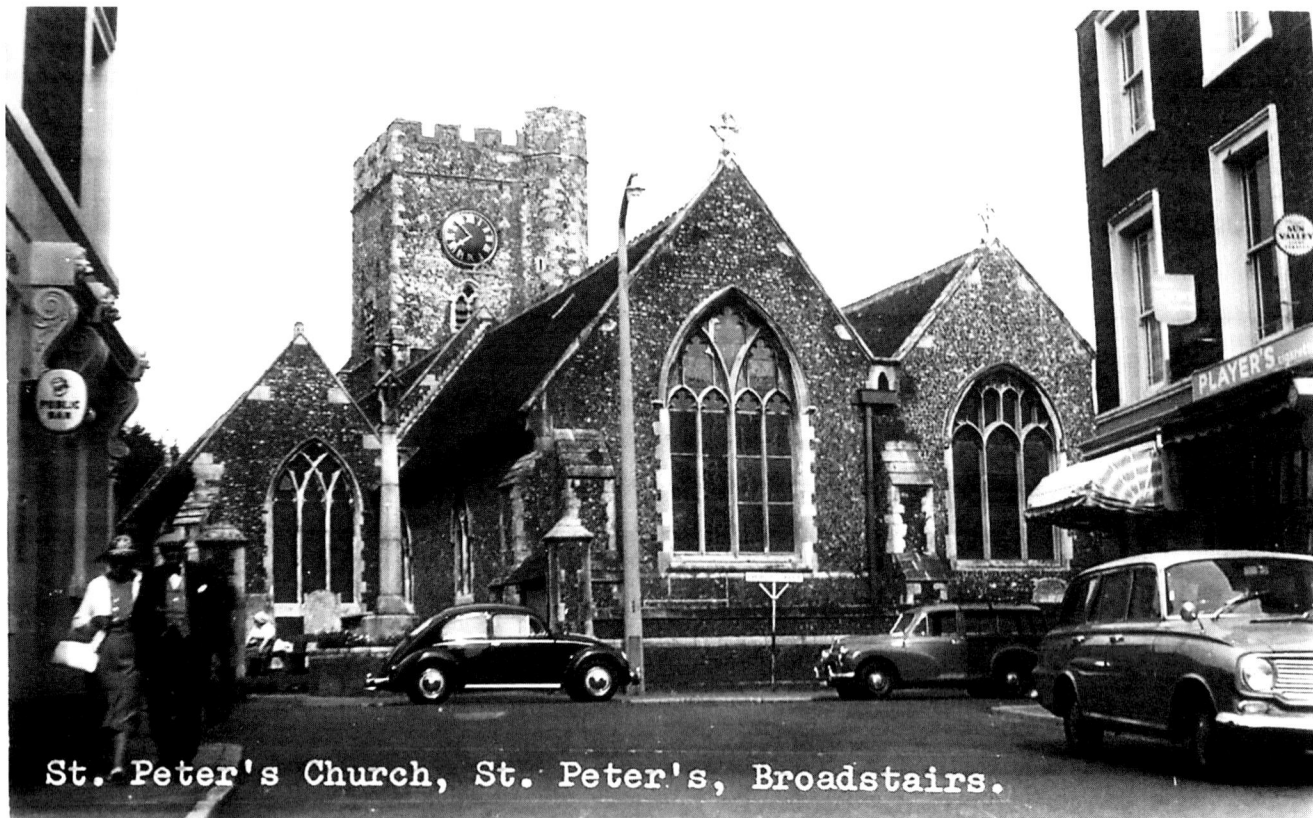

St. Peter's Church, St. Peter's, Broadstairs.

During the Napoleonic Wars the tower of St Peter's church was a naval lookout and is still allowed to fly the White Ensign today. Just inside its main gate is an 18th century memorial to Richard Joy, who until 2007, was thought to be the Kentish Samson, the strongest man in the county. It transpires that it was his brother William who had the title and he died while at sea in 1734.

The Ford Prefect car, also known as the Ford 100E, plants this photograph at the junction of St Peter's High Street with Church Street firmly into the mid 1950s. The village's medicinal needs were met by DT Evans, the chemist on the corner, while opposite, medicines of a different kind were on tap in the Red Lion, then a Tomson & Wotton house, which still exists.

The 11th century flint built parish church dominates in this 1909 view of St Peter's High Street. The pub on the left was the Crown & Thistle and dated from the 17th century. It was demolished in the 1950s to be replaced by two shops. The entrance to Jennings' butcher's can be seen on the right. Also set in the High Street used to be Creasy's slaughterhouse and adjoining grocery which was the only place in the village with an off sales licence for wines & spirits in the 1920s.

Ye New Wash House, Albion House, St. Peter's in Thanet.

The New Wash House wasn't a public bath but one of several hand laundries in the vicinity. Shirts and collars were a speciality. A rising platform appears to have been added to the extreme left hand window. The view dates from the early 20th century. By the 1930s Albion House had been converted into flats.

One of Broadstairs most notable residents was media baron Lord Northcliffe, the founder of the Daily Mail in 1896 and later owner of The Times. He lived at Elmwood, seen here in the late 1950s, in Reading Street village, from 1891 until his death as a Viscount in 1922, aged only 57. During the First World War, he was Minister for Propaganda. In February 1917, German destroyers tried to bombard the house but in doing so struck nearby Rose Cottage, killing a mother and two daughters. Recently, there has been speculation around whether the Germans were targeting Lord Northcliffe's home or merely shelling the Thanet area in general.

This idyllic scene of Reading Street is from a postcard sent in July 1939, two months before the start of the Second World War. Some girls are making their way along the road while an old lady watches from her front gate. The girls are just passing the Post Office on the left of the view where there is a phone box outside. Beyond is the tower of St Andrew's church, which faces The White Swan pub.

The Hearts of Oak Benefit Society built a brand new home for its members in 1938 on the site of Callis Court, the one time mansion of Harry H Marks MP in Callis Court Road. The home cost £50,000 to build and equip and provided for 50 convalescents in relaxing surroundings incorporating some of Callis Court's gardens. The home was redeveloped by the Royal British Legion which transferred residents of Maurice House, seven miles away at Westgate, to the new building in 1983 – the name of the home was carried over as well.

Along Convent Road heading towards Kingsgate, was Glyn House School, seen here, top, in the 1930s. Originally built in 1913 as Brondesbury Ladies' School for 'daughters of professional men', exams were optional. Both lower photos: By the 1960s, the site had been renamed Kingsgate College and was used mainly for teaching English to overseas students. From 1990 until 2018 it was part of Chaucer College, catering for Japanese students learning English. Following its £3 million auction sale, plans were announced in June 2020 to create 18 luxury apartments, a scheme approved by Thanet District Council in March 2021.

At Sunshine Coast's End – The Broadstairs Story

Port Regis, taking the Latin name for Kingsgate, was built in 1764 by eccentric landowner Lord Holland. Originally named the Convent of St Mildred, and hence its address in Convent Road, it was actually home to his retired estate workers. Seen here in a postcard from 1911, Port Regis later became a charitable institution offering shelter for poor women of the parish.

Port Regis became a boys' school in 1921 when bought by Sir Milsom Rees, King George V's laryngologist and in the years before World War Two William Joyce – later the infamous German radio propagandist Lord Haw Haw – taught English here.
From 1945 until the late 1970s Port Regis was run as a convent for 'delicate girls' by the Belgian order of the Daughters of the Cross. Today, Port Regis is a retirement home as well as a Montessori nursery school.

In seaside retirement on The Ranch

More than 85 years ago a five acre field in residential Broadstairs became the seaside retirement home for dozens of working horses and donkeys who would otherwise have met an unpleasant end.

Back in 1936 Miss Enid Briggs, her sister Phyllis and their mother, all keen animal lovers, bought some land in Sea View Road, to turn into an equine haven which they called simply, The Ranch.

The family was well established in Broadstairs and lived at North Foreland House overlooking the clifftop. Enid herself had built up a reputation as a keen film-maker in the 1920s and 1930s, recording on 16mm film many local events such as the annual water galas as well as shows by Uncle Mack's Minstrels, the troupe of black faced entertainers who performed song and dance routines. Much of her work is preserved in the Screen Archive South East collection.

The Briggs' philosophy was that once a horse was past

IN RETIREMENT AT THE RANCH, BROADSTAIRS.
CHARLIE, BRENDA, & TRIXIE

Charlie, Brenda and Trixie were the horses which featured in one of a series of 1950s postcards showing the idyllic life they led in the lush green fields of The Ranch in Sea View Road, Broadstairs.

its prime and no longer fit for work, it could enjoy unbridled freedom and rest in Broadstairs. That freedom included living life unshod – a blacksmith was on hand to remove the shoes from new arrivals.

Interviewed in early 1961 by local journalist Bill Evans as The Ranch marked its 25th anniversary, Miss Briggs said: "When an animal retires here he has nothing to do but eat, rest and enjoy himself. He will never be sold to an unknown fate."

Some people, she often thought, with the best will in the world, believe all they had to do for an animal in its old age is to give it some grass. But that wasn't enough for residents of The Ranch.

The home offered eight spacious paddocks and stables carpeted with straw. A meal of crushed oats and bran was provided twice a day for the animals. Hanging in the stable would also be a block of salt which the horses would enjoy licking.

Miss Briggs went on to say: "Most of our veterans have given up work because, as they are between 15 and 20 years old, their owners find they get tired easily and are never well.

"Some retire because they are lame or broken-winded, others have been in accidents, and a few others are here because they have proved too difficult to handle."

Some residents only reached The Ranch by the skin of their teeth. Two horses were once rescued from ships taking them abroad to be slaughtered. One was a

School groups were frequent visitors to The Ranch and it's Charlie who is getting all the attention from youngsters in this mid 1950s scene.

graceful black and white mare named Shamrock and an ex-tinker's pony called Neigh-Neigh.

They were rescued at the quayside as they were about to be exported but ladies from the Save the Irish Horses Fund bought them and sent them on to Broadstairs.

Another paddock was home for four former beach

donkeys but instead of being expected to give rides, as they might have done previously on the local beaches, they were the focus of youngsters' attention plying them with a variety of tit-bits.

"Our horses are of all sorts and sizes," said Miss Briggs. "There was Jasper, an old favourite who had lost his home through lack of grazing land and once had seven homes in three years. He made a contrasting picture with Dolly, a little Shetland pony he befriended.

Tommy, a newly retired London milk float horse, is unloaded from an animal ambulance at Victoria station to be transported by train to Broadstairs.

Dainty Dolly had lived a more routine life, having pulled a pony chaise along Ramsgate seafront for six years."

Very often, a new arrival to The Ranch wouldn't know how to react to the open, green surroundings. Miss Briggs said: "Some, after years of working in a town are at first overcome by the greenery and peace they find. Some horses have never been free in a paddock since they first went to work. The first thing they want to do is to roll. We had one old cart horse which, finding there was nobody to lead him and no cart to pull, just leaped into the air, taking all four feet off the ground. Then, not sure whether he had done right looked around and realising he wasn't going to be scolded – did it again!"

During the 1950s, some of the horses coming to The Ranch had pulled London milk floats and one called Tommy had done the job on the busy streets for 12 years. His first day was spent dashing around the place looking at everyone and everything, rolling in the grass and grazing. Going into his stable that night he tried to climb out of his box – evidently thinking his day in the paddock would be his last. Happily, handfuls of corn placated him.

Several London milkmen would make annual visits to The Ranch during their holidays to meet the horses they had once worked with on the capital's streets.

The first of the London milk horses to arrive in Broadstairs came from United Dairies stables at East Finchley and had worked hard for 10 years. A customer had long admired the black beast on his rounds and had asked to buy him when he retired but United Dairies didn't take her seriously.

When he was missed, he had already been sold to a farmer in Bedford. Luckily, the farmer was willing to sell him and sent him to Broadstairs, well supplied with food.

Later on, old farm horses and ex-riding school horses formed the main intake at The Ranch. These were animals which had been retired earlier than others thanks partly to replacement by vehicles and thanks to a more enlightened view of not working animals for too many years.

A firm rule of Miss Briggs was that once an owner had agreed to sell or donate their horse to The Ranch, there was no going back. Once retired, the animal would never know another home and when he had to meet his end, he would be humanely put down.

Hanging in Miss Briggs' office was a set of brasses which once belonged to a lovable old horse known as Bill. An old Southern Railway horse, he had been taken over by Miss Briggs before her family opened The Ranch. He was employed to carry hay from her home to The Ranch, pulling the first rubber tyred cart in the district.

One of the largest horses to become a resident in The Ranch's silver jubilee year was a 17 year old Clydesdale called Jock. Standing at a little over 16 hands high, he arrived in a horse box from Berkshire where his owner had

At Sunshine Coast's End – The Broadstairs Story

heard about The Ranch from a boy who had read a book about the place written by Miss Briggs.

The Ranch remained a popular destination for horses and donkeys for many years and it received many visitors – usually school groups or former workmates of the horses – several milkmen made annual outings for another chance to meet again with their four legged friends. Volunteers were never in short supply either to take day to day care of the residents.

Exactly when The Ranch closed is not clear but Miss Briggs died in 1973, aged 75, so it's quite possible the horses were rehomed elsewhere before the site was subsequently redeveloped to create the new houses of Rhodes Gardens, Dorcas Gardens and Radley Close.

Neigh-Neigh and Shamrock find their way back to the stable yard at the end of another day in retirement in 1961.

Miss Enid Briggs shows off brasses belonging to Bill, a former railway horse, to a group of schoolchildren during 1961.

Dr Tester – the North Foreland Nazi

Less than a quarter of a century after publication in 1915 of John Buchan's spy novel The 39 Steps – a tale of espionage inspired by a flight of stairs cut into the cliffs on Broadstairs North Foreland Estate, and used by the author while convalescing at a house nearby called St Cuby – than someone who was considered a threat to national security could have fled down them to a waiting vessel and be spirited off to a distant land.

We hark back to the late 1920s just as Adolf Hitler and the Nazi party were becoming a political force in Germany.

Arriving on these shores in late 1927 was one Dr Arthur Albert Tester. He was born in Stuttgart in 1895. He claimed, falsely as it turned out, to be the son of that city's British consul. He was not a medical doctor but said he had gained the title as a doctor of law in Germany and a doctor of philosophy in Belgium. He described himself though as a financier.

Dr Tester's passport photo, thought to be the only surviving image of him, is held on file at the Public Records Office, Kew.

In fact he was nothing more than a conman, working in league with others to make money by setting up spurious companies in Germany and Belgium, inviting people to invest in them, before making off with their considerable amounts of cash.

After setting up a bank in London in 1929, to watch it fail only a year later, Tester, his second wife Charlotte, and their six children settled in a large 20 room house named Naldera on the North Foreland Estate, for which he paid £6,000.

The house had been built as the retirement home of Lord Curzon, former Viceroy of India, at the turn of the twentieth century. He died in 1925 and Naldera had been left empty until the Testers moved in.

The house had been inherited by Lord Curzon's daughter, Lady Cynthia, who had married Sir Oswald Mosley in 1920. He would go on to form the British Union of Fascists and Dr Tester became one of its first members.

Dr Tester fully lived up to the part of the wealthy man about town. Expensively dressed, he was often seen with a cigar in one hand and a monocle over one eye. He became known around Broadstairs for his expensive taste in cars – a Rolls-Royce, a Spanish built Hispano Suiza and an American made Auburn were his principal choices of transport. By coincidence, the author's late father, then still a teenager, worked at Arter & Co's garage which maintained them (a Co-op store stands in its place now). Its customers also included local policemen who hinted at Dr Tester's home being kept under surveillance by the Secret Service.

Dr Tester could often be seen being chauffeur driven to the railway station to catch a train to his London office in St James' Place. The jackbooted retainer was as arrogant as his master, one local observed years later.

Dr Tester's sympathies for the Fascist movement were soon recognised – after all he had been telling people he was Mosley's aide-de-camp and was seen handing out BUF literature outside its branch office at 74 High Street, Broadstairs. A rightly suspicious media labelled him as the Englishman who spoke the language with a German accent.

But what really brought him to the attention of the Secret Service was a company he had set up with one Joseph Ruston, alias Joseph Hepburn-Ruston, called the European Press Agency. In March 1938 allegations were made in the Belgian Chamber of Deputies that this company had received, via German industrialists, £110,000 from Josef Goebbels, the Nazi propaganda minister, to buy a Brussels newspaper and turn it into an anti-communist mouthpiece.

Seen here in the summer of 2002 is the impressive house Naldera, on the North Foreland Estate, bought by Dr Tester for £6,000. The house is now divided into flats.

Following these claims the British media investigated the European Press Agency. It transpired that Ruston's London business address was the same as Dr Tester's at 14 St James' Place. A Daily Express reporter who visited the premises was told Dr Tester was not a director of the agency and denied any money was coming from Goebbels. It was later discovered the agency was run through the offices of Fritz Hesse, a London based press attaché working under Joachim von Ribbentrop, Germany's ambassador to Britain between 1936 and 1938.

Dr Tester later told an Express journalist he and Ruston were closely connected with the BUF adding: "I am a fascist and do not care who knows it."

The British Army On the Rhine had suspected Dr Tester as a dubious character as early as 1926. Below is an entry from a report about him, held at the Public Records Office, Kew, London.

He also told the newspaper: "I am Sir Oswald Mosely's personal aide-de-camp. I do not speak for him at public meetings because I cannot go around with a placard on my shoulder saying 'British born but for 20 years brought up in Germany', and that is why I speak English with a German accent."

Another company formed by Dr Tester and Ruston, called British Glycerine Manufacturers, was based in Gravesend and received a dawn visit from the authorities on the same grounds that it too was a front for siphoning German cash to the fascists.

Things finally got too hot for Dr Tester in late 1938, soon after the Munich crisis – when Prime Minister Neville Chamberlain declared 'peace in our time'.

Dr Tester had recently acquired the 250 feet long steam yacht Lucinda for £7,500 from a boat yard at Roehampton. Soon, the vessel had a crew of 24, costing £300 a week.

(i). Arthur TESTER, son of former British Consul in STUTTGART. Gives himself out to be an Englishman, but is actually of German nationality, like his father. He possesses a British passport. After posing throughout the war as a good German he has posed as a good Englishman ever since. He is a notorious rogue, blackmailer and swindler.

On Christmas Eve 1938 the Lucinda was seen in Southampton Water picking up passengers – the Tester family and his associates – and sailing for the Mediterranean, ostensibly for a Christmas cruise but in reality this was a voyage to Port Said in Egypt and the Suez Canal. Back at home, MI5 was by now on Dr Tester's case and building up information about his expected return in April 1939.

April came and went without the Lucinda showing up in Southampton. Enquiries revealed the vessel was in dry dock in Naples and several of the crew had returned to England, fed up of Dr Tester's anti-British talk. Ever the businessman, Dr Tester spent the next few months trying to pull together deals around fine wines.

A painting of the 250 feet long steam yacht Lucinda, aboard which Dr Tester and his family made good their escape from Britain as war clouds were gathering.

The outbreak of war in September saw the Lucinda sail for Greece where Dr Tester's wife and children disembarked. He sailed on to Port Said and apparently handed over the cruiser to the Royal Navy before returning a couple of months later to Greece.

He then spent a year or so setting up front companies in the region, trying to undermine British interests, before making his way to Romania to become involved with the German military intelligence organisation, the Abwehr.

He is reported to have lived at Castle Mintia, near Dava, and to have been given the codename Teddy.

Whether true or not, he was certainly involved in interrogating – and party to the subsequent likely torture of – British Special Operations Executive agents captured during a commando operation in 1943 in Romania which had gone badly wrong.

Other reports suggest Dr Tester infiltrated a Macedonian resistance movement which was planning an overthrow of the country's German-backed government, as well as countering a Greek resistance group supported by the British.

He managed to avoid interrogation by the Germans themselves, who were becoming increasingly wary of his motives, seeing Dr Tester as nothing more than a war profiteer.

Perhaps not surprisingly, Dr Tester appears to have come to a sticky end. It is said he was fleeing Romania in late September 1944 when he was shot and killed at the border with Hungary by a guard somewhere near the town of Arad.

His car was riddled with bullet holes as it fell down an embankment and caught fire. A body was found alongside the car at the bottom with personal effects which suggested it was Dr Tester. But it was claimed he had staged the whole scenario himself and had slipped away by another route to Budapest using a passport personally signed by Adolf Hitler. Not long after, that part of the world was occupied by the Russians.

In 1945 Special Branch called on the recently demobbed Ramsgate dentist Brigadier J Morley Stebbings – Dr Tester had been a patient of his before the war – and took away x-rays of Tester's jaw.

Nine years later Dr Tester was declared legally dead in the High Court after the jaw from the corpse – exhumed by the Russians at British request – was found to match the dentist's x-rays. This decision enabled members of his family to finally claim what was left of his estate, thought to be worth about £25,000 at the time.

Naldera had been abandoned since Dr Tester left in 1938 and it had been broken into and looted on several occasions after. Apparently, pictures, furniture and silverware had all disappeared yet a lot of pro BUF literature and a black silk shirt were untouched. However, a public auction of the house and its remaining contents in the mid 1950s realised £8,000. A life size portrait of Hitler went unsold.

An October 1972 news report from the Kent Messenger suggests Dr Tester would have been appointed Gauleiter of Kent had there been a successful German invasion of Britain in 1940.

The Nazi who would have ruled Kent

BY KEN BINDOFF

A RECENT book and TV programme has started a big argument of interest in what life would have been like in Britain if the Germans had won the war. Because of its close proximity to Europe, Kent inevitably would have been the first part of England to feel the Nazi jackboot after defeat. The Germans prepared for this 10 years before the start of the Second World War. They sent to Kent a man they felt would play a leading part in the terror, oppression and mass deportations Hitler in-

tended to inflict on us. Now he is to figure in a book which is to be written in Brussels abour the Gestapo chief who would have had life and death powers over everybody who survived in Kent after we had been defeated. Needless to say, I had no idea of the sinister purpose behind Dr. Albert Tester's residence in Kent when I met him shortly after his move to Broadstairs. Dr. Tester — it was a legal qualification — lived with his blonde wife, Charlotte, and their five children, at a

clifftop mansion called Naldera immediately below North Foreland lighthouse. At first the British Secret Service appears to have displayed little more than a routine interest in the events taking shape on the Kent coast. But as Europe moved nearer to war official curiosity increased. Charlotte and the children returned to Germany during the summer of 1939. A few days before the outbreak of war the authorities decided to detain Dr. Tester under 18B. Police who went to arrest

him found the house deserted and in darkness. Nobody can be sure how the monacled doctor made his hurried exit from Britain, but he is thought to have escaped

by boat from the beach at the foot of the North Foreland cliffs. The generally accepted theory is that he was rowed out from the lonely beach one night and taken on board a U-boat lurking offshore in the darkness.

The next time he came to my mind was in the summer of 1945. I was going through a file of army intelligence reports on the activities of the Gestapo.

One concerned an incident in Rumania in 1944 when a senior German official found himself surrounded by advancing Russians at a place called Castle Mintia.

The official, who answered the description of the German doctor I had known casually at

Broadstairs, had tried to break out, but had found that all the roads through the forest were blocked.

He was shot and killed when his car swerved and plunged into a ditch after smashing through a wooden road barrier.

At our request the Russians exhumed the body. But more than a year had passed and the only possible method of identification was if we could match up dental charts.

Security men with details of the dead Gestapo official's teeth made a systematic check on

Thanet dentists, seeking one who might have treated Dr. Tester and who might still know his case history.

The search ended at Ramsgate, where the late Brigadier J. Morley Stebbings had recently returned to his dental practice after looking the Royal harbour.

Brigadier Stebbings, whose daughter, Mrs. Angela Cobb, is a member of KCC, had treated Dr. Tester during the time he lived at Broadstairs. He was able to provide the proof we needed.

109   *At Sunshine Coast's End – The Broadstairs Story*

Botany Bay, Kingsgate & the Foreland

Chalk stacks standing on their own, separate from the cliffs of Botany Bay – Broadstairs' most westerly beach – make an impressive sight today. However, back in the 1950s when Sunbeam Photography captured this image, the erosion which wore away the cliffs had barely started and only a comparatively small archway was to be found here.

This is Fitzroy Avenue, Kingsgate, probably in the late 1920s or early 1930s and was one of a profusion of pleasant avenues that sprang up in the area during the first three decades of the 20th century when people continued to move to the coast for bracing sea air and sunshine. Bungalows have long since gobbled up the open land on the right but there is still an unhurried atmosphere here. Today, some properties in this road command sale prices of more than £750,000.

At Sunshine Coast's End – The Broadstairs Story

Kingsgate Avenue.

Kingsgate Avenue was originally built to appeal to the professional and upper middle classes and is seen here around 1930. Dogs and walkers were safe to roam in the middle of the traffic free road. The properties in the centre distance are in Percy Avenue. Again, there has been considerable development over the decades, both of apartment blocks and larger houses.

1875 - 1961
FRANK RICHARDS
CREATOR OF
BILLY BUNTER
LIVED HERE

A sole Austin trundles along Percy Avenue, pictured just prior to the Second World War. The road was named after Percy Snowden who developed parts of the area and built these detached houses for a middle class clientele. However, inset: 131, Rose Lawn, stands out with a blue plaque to Frank Richards, the pen name of Charles Hamilton, who lived there for 30 years, and was the creator of owlish schoolboy Billy Bunter and friends at Greyfriars School.

Left: Charles Hamilton's house Rose Lawn, seen here in 2007, came up for sale in 2021 for £485,000 via a local estate agent.
Right: The author is pictured wearing trademark skull cap while lighting his pipe. When he died in late 1961, his housekeeper Edith Hood phoned local journalist Bill Evans asking 'Do you think anyone would be interested?' The story soon made international headlines! Charles Hamilton is reputed to have written about seven million words in his many books, more than any author.

The old flint Tower. Kingsgate.

Hoare's Series.

Walkers along the clifftop between Fayreness and the Captain Digby pub will be familiar with the Arx Rouchim, originally built of flint by Lord Holland as one of his many follies. Modelled on King Henry VIII's castle at Deal, it is also known as the Temple of Neptune or Neptune's Tower. Inset: The old tower has long since collapsed, leaving the outer Arx standing alone. A coastguard hut also stood here until sometime in the 1920s but now the Arx provides a convenient windbreak for golfers.

The "Captain Digby" Hotel & Bay, Kingsgate-on-Sea.

The Noble Captain Digby was built between 1763 and 1768 as another of Lord Holland's follies. It was originally half of the Bede House, which fell into the sea in 1809. Steps nearby led to the beach and were used by smugglers. By 1909 tea parties were being catered for "in any number at short notice". Note the proximity of the Arx Rouchim on the clifftop with the coastguard hut beside it in this view captured during the mid 1920s.

"Captain Digby" Hotel, Kingsgate-on-Sea

The pub was named after Lord Holland's favourite nephew who built a navy career catching smugglers. Shrimp brand beers were for sale in the 1930s and were advertised prominently on one side of the building. The Captain Digby was bought in 1979 by Frank Thorley as one of his first pubs and is still part of the Thorley Taverns estate.

Lord Holland, who lived in the large white house partly seen on the right hand edge of this Sunbeam photo, wanted to awaken to a view of a castle – so in 1766 he commissioned the most spectacular of his nine follies, Kingsgate Castle, which he used as his stables and accommodation for the grooms. It is seen here from the Captain Digby terrace sometime in the 1950s.

KINGSGATE CASTLE.

Extensive alterations were made to upgrade the accommodation of Kingsgate Castle during the 1860s and 1903. Lord Avebury, who introduced the Bank Holiday, was a subsequent owner. Reuben Peace purchased the place from Lady Avebury in 1922, after her husband's death, to run it as a smart hotel. Its summertime fancy dress balls were very popular in this era. The castle was converted into 32 privately owned flats during the 1950s.

Pictured soon after its opening in 1957, the Castle Keep Hotel was built on a neighbouring plot to Kingsgate Castle but was a separate entity. The best of its 20 bedrooms were available on weekly terms for 22 guineas (£23.10) at the time. Bed and breakfast was at least one guinea (£1.05). The hotel was extended during the 1970s to offer 40 bedrooms along with a large open air swimming pool. The owners at the time were Peter and Pat Stoneham who successfully built up the business into what became Thanet's only three star hotel. Swish cabaret evenings were a popular feature by the middle of the decade.

Come on in, the water's lovely, could be the caption to this 1975 press picture of two bathing belles enjoying Castle Keep's new pool. There was little doubt this was one of the best places for a dip in the area. Many showbiz stars stayed at the hotel when appearing in local theatres including Morecambe & Wise and Larry Grayson. Castle Keep closed in the late 1990s and eventually the site was redeveloped into smart apartment blocks between 2007 and 2010, all of which offer panoramic views overlooking the sea.

Taken in May 2015, this aerial photo gives us a good indication of the scale of the buildings forming Kingsgate Castle and the adjoining blocks of apartments which replaced the Castle Keep Hotel. The road running diagonally from the top left corner of the view is Joss Gap Road and beyond it is part of North Foreland golf course. Promenades help ensure the cliff is well protected from coastal erosion.

Kingsgate and Joss Bays feature in this scene, also captured from about 1,500 feet in May 2015. At the top of the frame we can make out part of the North Foreland Estate and North Foreland Road which leads up hill to the lighthouse. Below that are Joss Bay, the golf course and Kingsgate Castle before meeting Kingsgate Bay and the Captain Digby pub, with its car park, at the bottom.

Contrary to popular belief, Joss Bay does not get its name from smuggler Joss Snelling, but is more likely to be the other way around. The bay, seen here as a popular sun trap in the 1930s, was used by the tenants of what was Joss Farm for collecting seaweed in the 17th century, before Snelling was born. Coastal erosion has taken its toll on the cliffs during the decades since, with sand being swept higher up on the unprotected parts by the motions of the tide.

It was at Joss Bay that the very first attempts at developing radar, known as listening ears or sound mirrors, were made during the First World War in hope of detecting enemy aircraft approaching across the sea. It's not clear how successful were the trials but years later much larger sound mirrors were built near Dungeness on the Romney Marsh before radar became viable in time for the Second World War.

Sunbeam Photography caught this image of the lost art of thatching a hayrick at Elmwood Farm, in the beam of North Foreland lighthouse, during the late 1950s. In the days long before farmers vacuum-packed straw for animal feed, thatching a hayrick was vital to keep dry the following winter's cattle feed and fodder. Until the middle of the 20th century, up to half of all thatching carried out in Britain was this type of work – and proved invaluable in helping keep alive a traditional craft skill.

This postcard of an undulating North Foreland golf course was used in June 1952. Looking from somewhere near the top of Joss Gap Road, we can make out one end of North Foreland Estate, on the extreme left, and the lighthouse with one of its radio masts alongside. The golf club was founded in 1903 after the first course was laid out by Sir William Capel Slaughter, founder of international law practice Slaughter & May. After he died, Lord Northcliffe, by now living at Elmwood in Reading Street, purchased and enlarged the course as well as building a single storey clubhouse in Convent Road. North Foreland Golf Club thrives to this day.

North Foreland showing Lighthouse & Cliffs.

There has been a beacon shone from North Foreland since 1499, making it the oldest light still in use in England. The present one was built in 1691 but has been considerably altered since. The lighthouse, pictured in the 1920s soon after it was electrified, is around 90 feet tall. It was the last in the UK to be permanently manned until 26 November 1998 when it was switched over to automatic operation at a ceremony attended by the Duke of Edinburgh. The lighthouse's main beam is visible for 19 sea miles.

Inset: Royal Mail took the chance to launch a set of lighthouse stamps here in March 1998 with a local postie and the keeper.

Virtually opposite the lighthouse was the Dutch Tea House. Originally the North Foreland Tea House, it was a pleasant place for a cuppa after a bracing walk from the centre of Broadstairs. Waitresses in Dutch costume attended customers. Open all year round, it was doubling as a sub Post Office in 1956. The Dutch Tea House also took in paying guests and by the mid 1950s offered terms from eight guineas (£8.40) per week, quite pricey when other guest houses were often charging £1 per person less. These days the building has reverted to a private house, secluded by tall hedges and trees.

Broadstairs has been home to numerous private schools including St Stephen's College, one of few catering solely for girls. It was established in 1867 and moved to its premises in North Foreland Road at the end of the 1960s. In 1970 gifts of Arabian horses were made to the school by Major General Nasser, brother-in-law of King Hussein of Jordan. Below: Headmistress Miss Joan Selby-Lowndes has unloaded one of the newly arrived animals from its box in front of an admiring crowd.

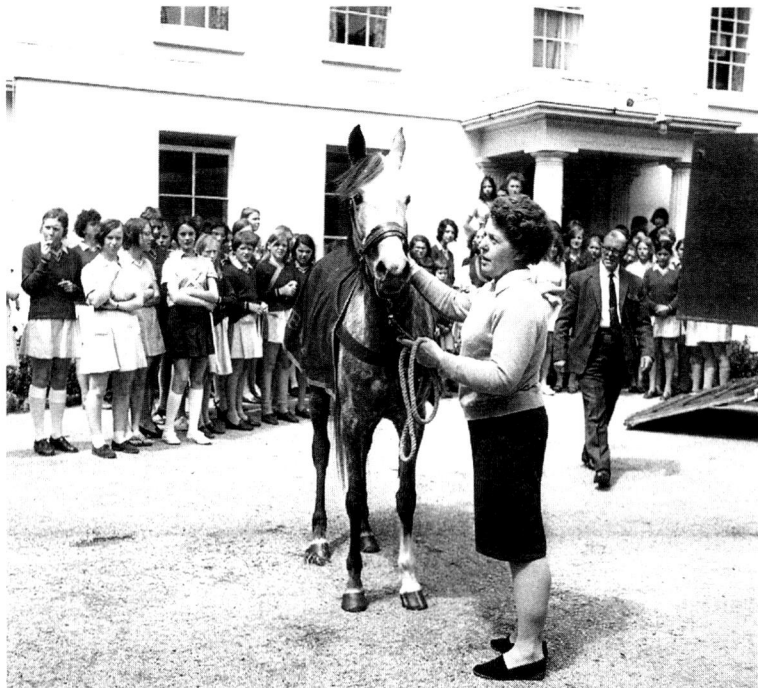

Above: The Major General's daughters, Zein, Nour and Rajha, were pupils at the school and were quick to welcome the horses to St Stephen's. The animals went a long way to establishing a successful riding school for the 125 college pupils. Primary age girls were boarded at a house named Wynstow, across the road from St Stephen's, and used a tunnel to get to and from the main buildings each day.

Here we see the younger pupils of Form Two during an English lesson in 1970. By the time St Stephen's closed in 1991, girls from all over the world had passed through its gates. The site was derelict for some years but eventually made way for the houses of Foreland Heights. This development was later followed by the creation of the attractive Broadhall Manor apartments block on ground formerly occupied by the stables.

On the Broadstairs side of the North Foreland Estate, in Stone Road, is Thanet Place, the former home of meat millionaire Sir Edmund Vestey who, with his brother William, formed the Blue Star Shipping Line and the Union Cold Storage Co to become one of the wealthiest families in the country by the early 20th century. The Italianate style palace was completed in 1929 for £100,000. This view was captured in 1958, five years after Sir Edmund's death, just as St Mary's Children's Home was established here. The building still stands but its seven acre grounds, inset, have been built on to create Thanet Place Gardens and Elizabeth Court.

THE INVALIDS SHELTER, RECTORY ROAD, BROADSTAIRS

A public shelter – or invalids shelter, as the postcard describes it – is an unusual focus of attention in this 1950s scene. Quite why it was chosen is not easy to fathom but we have a good view along Rectory Road, devoid of parked cars and looking towards the sea on a quiet day. The road gets its name from the fact the rectory to Holy Trinity Church was built here in 1871. These days Copperfield Court, a block of flats, occupies the site of the once prestigious Esplanade Hotel.

For decades, the shop to the left of this view has been a local landmark. What was once Dawson's newsagent marked the descent of Ramsgate Road meeting Queen's Road, curving away to the left, and York Street, branching to the right. The well worn post box is placed on the corner of Wrotham Road, which leads down to Victoria Parade.

THE VALE, BROADSTAIRS
L 2335

The Vale, formerly The Lynch, and off Ramsgate Road, was home of the Collegiate School in the 1860s, a high class establishment for young ladies and gentlemen. The spire of the congregational church can be clearly seen in this 1950s view which also shows a number of guest houses along the same side of the road. The Vale took on its name when houses forming Inverness Terrace, further along on the left, were built for the servants of Princess, later Queen, Victoria when she stayed at Pierremont Hall.

The Yarrow Home, fronting Ramsgate Road, was originally a children's convalescent home established by shipbuilder and philanthropist Sir Alfred Yarrow in 1894 for £35,000 to care for up to 100 youngsters of the 'better classes' recovering from illness. The weekly fee then was five shillings (25p). By the mid 1960s, the building had become Thanet Technical College which quickly built a solid reputation for excellence in catering and hospitality industry training courses. In 2016, the building saw completion of a three year project to turn it into the Yarrow Hotel, the only hotel set within the grounds of a further education establishment. Offering 28 bedrooms, five suites, restaurant, bars and solarium, it was awarded four star status in 2018.

Variously a military hospital during two world wars and still used as a children's home until the 1960s, the Jacobean style building was grade two listed in 1998 after a member of staff discovered plans to demolish it to make way for a modern teaching block. The Yarrow building was mothballed in 2011 until the plans were agreed to create the Yarrow Hotel two years later.

The spy who twisted his combinations!

On a September day in 1935, recently widowed Florence Johnson was glad she had been able to rent her furnished bungalow to such a pleasant couple.

True, Germans were unusual among Broadstairs holidaymakers but the lawyer-novelist from Hamburg and his pretty young niece seemed so glad to find a place by the sea where they could take a break during their motorcycle tour of England.

They had been sent by the house agents and asked if it was convenient to view Havelock, 6 Stanley Road, right away (the bungalow was later renamed Rosevine). They seemed charmed with everything, including the garden and the outhouse in which Dr Hermann Goertz could keep his motorbike and sidecar combination. They said it was perfect and agreed to take it for six weeks – possibly longer.

It was also agreed that Mrs Johnson, who lived nearby, should call by a couple of times a week to tend the garden. The couple moved in six days later having ridden their

Pictured in the late 1970s, the bungalow Havelock, in Stanley Road, provided an ideal retreat for Dr Hermann Goertz and his niece Marianne Emig for nearly six weeks in 1935.

Zundapp motorbike and sidecar from Mildenhall in Suffolk.

Dr Goertz was 45 years old, finely built with two sabre marks on his cheek, apparently from duelling. They made a great fuss of Mrs Johnson's terrier Tommy when she visited them, the girl saying he was beautiful.

Though they couldn't converse well, for Marianne Emig

Dr Hermann Goertz, pictured soon after his arrest at Harwich in late 1935.

The doctor was usually reading papers in the conservatory or cleaning his motorbike and she found them an extremely happy pair.

The six weeks were nearly up when, unexpectedly, Mrs Johnson received a telegram from Dr Goertz, sent from Dover. It said they had gone to Germany for a few days. It added: "Take care of my combination and photo", and was signed 'Gorby'. The following day she had a postcard from Ostend asking her to take care of his bicycle combination.

He hadn't returned when his tenancy was up and when Mrs Johnson and the house agent went into the bungalow to check the inventory she found the photo and a camera but couldn't find the motorcycle and sidecar. Thinking it stolen, she called the police.

"Then we found a pair of soiled white overalls. And suddenly we realised these were what he called his combinations," she said.

But there was more than that.

spoke little English, Mrs Johnson was impressed by her beauty.

"Sometimes when I entered the garden she would be whistling like a bird, sometimes singing, sometimes playing a mouth organ – she was as happy as a schoolgirl," Mrs Johnson would say later.

Owner of Havelock, Florence Johnson with her terrier Tommy. The spies adored the pet when they turned up in Broadstairs during the late summer of 1935.

There were documents and papers of more than passing interest, details and drawings of RAF bases. In one pocket of the overalls was a tiny but elaborate camera. When processed, its film revealed negatives the size of a postage stamp of airfields and aircraft in flight.

Dr Goertz returned alone to Britain three weeks later and was promptly arrested on arrival at Harwich on 8 November. Later in the month, the country read a shock War Office statement saying he had been charged under the Official Secrets Act. One charge related to 'another person not in custody' – for Marianne Emig never returned to these shores.

Initial court proceedings were held in Margate – the first of their kind in Britain since the First World War – and attracted a lot of local and national press attention despite some of the case being held behind closed doors on grounds of national security.

The Isle of Thanet Gazette reported at the end of November 1935 that: "A German girl alleging to have asked a young Broadstairs airman for photographs of aeroplanes and aerodromes, a sketch of Manston Aerodrome found in the bungalow at Broadstairs, with documents mentioning the German intelligence service, provided sensational evidence when Dr Hermann Goertz was charged with espionage at the Cinque Ports Petty Sessions, Margate.

"Dozens of newspaper reporters and photographers from London caused excitement in the quiet market square by wandering around the Town Hall trying to seek admission to the court before proceedings began. The doors were closely guarded and police officers shielded Goertz from the merciless battery of cameras when he walked to the court from the Metropolitan Police van in which he was brought from Brixton prison.

"There was a ripple of excitement in court when Goertz ascended

The hastily hand-written postcard message sent to Florence Johnson by Dr Hermann Goertz.

the stairs from the police station and entered the dock. Keen-eyed, he was quite unlike the square-headed prototype with which English imagination associates the German race."

The Gazette went on to add that the young woman was Marianne Emig, said to be Dr Goertz's niece. While they were in Broadstairs, they became friendly with a young airman, Kenneth Lewis, who was at home on leave from the RAF's base at Lee-on-Solent.

The prosecution told magistrates the airman visited the bungalow when Dr Goertz and Marianne showed great interest in any matters relating to the air force. Marianne, perhaps in a bid to allay his misgivings about parting with information, said: 'You must remember that in the next war England and Germany will be on the same side.'

She told the airman she would be willing to pay for films or photos of any RAF machines he could provide. She invited him to Germany saying she might be able to help him financially. Among others things, she asked the airman to always write on RAF crested stationery and to destroy any letters he might get in reply.

When Dr Goertz was picked up at Harwich, three letters from the airman to Marianne were found in his possession along with postcard and cigarette card photos of aircraft he had sent with them.

During their stay in Stanley Road, Dr Goertz and his niece attracted some attention among the neighbours. The pair were seen going out most days on their motorbike with Marianne usually driving and Dr Goertz

The telegram message sent by Dr Hermann Goertz which sparked a frantic search for his motorcycle combinations.

riding pillion. Occasionally, Dr Goertz would ride alone to venture into the town centre.

The magistrates remanded Dr Goertz in custody at Brixton prison, ahead of a full trial at London's Old Bailey in February and March 1936. There, he was accused of 'making a sketch, plan or note of RAF Manston, calculated to be useful to an enemy and conspiring with Marianne Emig to commit offences under the Official Secrets Act.'

Denying the charge, he claimed he had come to England to research material for a novel. The Old Bailey trial would see three witnesses give evidence 'in camera' (behind closed doors, with the public barred). Dr Goertz was found guilty and jailed for four years with hard labour.

It was thought Dr Goertz was not an official spy but was striving to show his friends in German intelligence what he could do by collecting information on his own initiative. His aim was to land a job in the German secret service, for which he had the advantage of speaking good English. He knew London and the Home Counties and had been an interrogator of crashed British airmen during World War One.

Dr Goertz served his time at Maidstone prison and, with permission, was released back to Germany in July 1939, two months before the start of the Second World War.

Despite his blunder over the use of the word combination, it seems the German espionage machine was prepared to overlook the error.

While in jail, he had met members of the Irish

GERMAN WHO IS ACCUSED OF SPYING

Exclusive "Daily Sketch" Picture Received Last Night From Hamburg

How the news of Goertz' arrest was carried by a national newspaper. Pictured with him, the girl he called his niece —Marianne Emig, 19

Photos of spies are not easy to come by – but the Daily Sketch managed to get hold of photos of both Dr Hermann Goertz and Marianne Emig from Hamburg.

Republican Army and in May 1940 Goertz was parachuted into the Republic of Ireland – a neutral country.

He jumped from a Heinkel bomber over Ballivor in Co Meath complete with US$20,000 in his coat, to keep

Dr Hermann Goertz's funeral was held in Dublin after his suicide there in 1947. His coffin was draped with a Nazi flag.

His presence in the Republic of Ireland caused a good deal of embarrassment to the authorities – working hard to preserve the country's neutrality – who narrowly missed catching him on at least one occasion in Dublin. Dr Goertz was finally rounded up in November 1941, more than 18 months after his arrival, and jailed at Athlone.

Dr Goertz tried to bribe a guard to relay messages for him via a Dublin café but instead the guard alerted his superiors. They advised him to go along with the scheme which enabled Irish intelligence to read the messages Goertz thought were being sent to Berlin. To keep up appearances, intelligence replied to Goertz in German telling him he had been promoted to the rank of major.

When the war ended, Dr Goertz was eventually released and started making plans to spend his remaining days in the republic but in 1947 he was rearrested and told he was being deported to Allied occupied Germany. Despite an assurance he would not be handed over to the Russians on arrival, Dr Goertz couldn't face the prospect of returning to the fatherland. He promptly swallowed a cyanide tablet in the Aliens' Office of Dublin Castle after being handed his papers. Nothing could be done to save him.

A short time after, Dr Goertz was buried in Luftwaffe officer uniform at Dublin's Dean Grange cemetery, the coffin draped with a Nazi Swastika flag.

him going for a few years, and a radio transmitter to stay in touch with Berlin. He soon made contact with the IRA and spent a long time trying to work up plans about potential German cooperation in attacks on Northern Ireland and a possible invasion codenamed Operation Kathleen.

Acknowledgements

The author would like to thank the following for their invaluable help:

Mrs Marian Evans for the loan of her postcard collection used extensively throughout the book
Broadstairs Folk Week for use of the photograph on page 9, taken by the Isle of Thanet Gazette
The Morelli family for use of the photographs on pages 21 and 22
Margate Museum for use of the photograph with Annette Mills on page 23
SEAS Heritage Collection © Thanet District Council for use of the photos on pages 69, 78, 79, 110, 118 and 126
Railway Images UK for use of the photo on page 72
Thanet Hidden History Facebook page for use of the photos on pages 125 and 129
Kent Photo Archive for the use of the photo on page 137.

Contemporary photographs © Nick Evans. All other photographs are © Bill Evans Collection.
They must not be reproduced without prior reference to the publisher.

Bibliography

Kelly's Isle of Thanet Directories 1934, 1938 and 1951
AA Hotel Handbook 1938, AA Members' Handbook 1957 and RAC Guide & Handbook 1958
Broadstairs official guides 1946, 1953 and 1956
The Story of Broadstairs & St Peter's by James Bird 1974
Old Broadstairs by Michael David Mirams 1986
Broadstairs & St Peter's In Old Photographs by John Whyman 1990
Early Broadstairs & St Peter's by Barrie Wootton 1992
Numerous cuttings and other items held by the Bill Evans Collection from publications including:
Isle of Thanet Gazette, Thanet Times, East Kent Times and Kent Life.

We have taken all reasonable steps to ensure the correct people are credited for their photographs but any issues can be addressed to bygonepublishing@gmail.com and amendments will be considered for any future editions.